AN INTRODUCTION TO
MUSICAL HISTORY

Music

AN INTRODUCTION TO
MUSICAL HISTORY

Sir Jack Westrup

HUTCHINSON OF LONDON

Hutchinson & Co (Publishers) Ltd
3 Fitzroy Square, London W1

London Melbourne Sydney Auckland
Wellington Johannesburg and agencies
throughout the world

First published 1955
Reprinted 1958, 1961, 1963, 1967 and 1970
2nd edition 1973
Reprinted 1978
© This edition J. A. Westrup 1973

Printed in Great Britain by litho at The Anchor Press Ltd
and bound by Wm Brendon & Son Ltd
both of Tiptree, Essex

ISBN 0 09 031592 8 (paper)

To Howard,
who has heard it all before

CONTENTS

PREFACE

THIS is not a history of music. It is simply an attempt to outline some of the problems which historians and students have to face, and to give some idea of the conditions in which music has come into existence. It is assumed that the reader has some musical background, since without it the study of musical history would be a complete waste of time. Quotations are for the most part taken from works which are easily accessible, but I have not hesitated, when necessary, to draw on other sources with which I happen to be familiar.

The proofs have been read by Professor Gerald Abraham, who has made a number of valuable suggestions. He will, I am sure, forgive me if I have not been able to adopt them all. Another debt which I have to acknowledge is to the University of Cape Town. A substantial part of the book was written while I was lecturing there in the spring of 1954. Its progress owes a great deal to the hospitality shown me by the University and to the kindness which I received from so many friends.

November 1954   J. A. WESTRUP

CHAPTER I

THE SCOPE OF MUSICAL HISTORY

WE can best understand the particular problems of the history of music by considering the nature of history in general. It is not merely a chronicle. The historian tries to treat events in an orderly sequence, to see patterns without imposing them, to study causes, results and the interactions of events, and finally to make all this interesting and stimulating to the reader. If we accept these four objectives there is no need to argue whether history is a science or an art. It is both —a science involving method and an art involving creative skill in presentation. It must inevitably select from a mass of material; and for that reason, however impartial it may be in intention, it must remain personal. We read the great historians—Gibbon and Macaulay, for example—not simply for what they tell us, which may be out of date or inaccurate, but for themselves.

If we now ask ourselves what the history of music is, it may be easier to answer the question by deciding first what it is not. It is not simply a record of composers, though many old-fashioned histories are content with this. It is still possible to find in second-hand bookshops works designed for popular consumption in which the names of composers are dutifully printed in black type. Many of these names are of little importance or interest, and many of them, one suspects, were little more than names to the authors. The uselessness of histories of this kind hardly needs demonstration. Even such an enlightened compilation as the *Handbuch der Musikgeschichte* edited by Guido Adler includes a section on the barren subject of nineteenth-century opera in England which consists simply of a page and a half of names and works; and an English historian, Henry Davey, in the second edition of his *History of English Music* (1921), is content to give Delius a single sentence, in which he tells us that he was "of German parentage" and "highly esteemed by many".

Nor is the history of music a mere account of musical activities or organizations, such as the Chapel Royal in England, the Mannheim orchestra in the eighteenth century, or the theatre built for Wagner's operas at Bayreuth. All these things are important as the soil in which music flourished, and they may very well have had a fruitful and lasting effect on musical composition. But they do not in themselves constitute a history of music: they serve rather to illustrate it. It is equally mistaken to think of the history of music as a series of movements, such as the rise of opera, romanticism, impressionism or nationalism. The answer to our question is, in fact, more general. The history of music is the history of an art which develops.

Such development is not necessarily in a straight line. Oriental and European music, for example, have pursued quite different paths, and their interactions have been negligible. For this reason it is possible to argue, as some writers have done, that there is no such thing as a history of "music" in the singular: we should speak rather of a history of "musics". This view finds some support in the fact that Oriental music is rarely intelligible to Europeans. At the same time it is quite possible that prolonged study and familiarity would make it perfectly intelligible; and even without this its technique is intelligible enough. It will, however, simplify the problem if we confine ourselves, as many modern historians do, to European music. Here, so far as our knowledge goes, it is quite reasonable to speak of a history of "music" in the singular. (The qualification is important: we do not know Greek music, for example, we know only its theory and that imperfectly.) Within the sphere of European music the music of one age is not necessarily a strange art to another. Plainsong is not a dead language: it is still sung and enjoyed. Many of the songs of the troubadours present no obstacle to the ordinary listener. The survival of folksong is another instance, and so is the popularity of Bach with music-lovers who know nothing whatever of the purposes for which his music was written. If we go to a concert which includes works of widely different periods we are still conscious of hearing specimens of the same art. Each age will hear these works differently, but that is quite another problem.

Development implies continuity. This is inevitable, since at no period can entirely new conventions be satisfactorily established. The fundamental nature of any art is always familiar, and each stage in its history profits from the last. But continuity does not necessarily imply either continuous development from simple to complex, or progress from a lower to a higher level. Development from simple to complex may indeed occur, but the reverse often happens. A song by Purcell is simpler than a Mass by Byrd; Stravinsky's texture is simpler than Wagner's. Complexity inevitably provokes reaction. For that matter the terms "simple" and "complex" are often ambiguous and need precise definition before they can be applied satisfactorily to individual works of art. The idea that music progresses as it develops is even more illusory. Is eighteenth-century music "better" than the music of the sixteenth century, is Vaughan Williams a "better" composer than Beethoven? The absurdity of this doctrine hardly needs argument. Yet it was at one time widely accepted, largely as a result of evolutionary theory in the nineteenth century. The truth is simple: a masterpiece is a masterpiece whenever it was written. There is no objection whatever to speaking of the "evolution" of music, but we shall get into great difficulties if we regard it as synonymous with progress. At the same time we need not pretend that there have not been ups and downs in the history of music. There have been times without any really great men, and there have been countries without great men for long periods. It has even been maintained, though with less justice, that great men have sometimes been active at "unhappy" periods, when circumstances were unfavourable to the development of their genius.[1]

The history of music stresses a changing continuity, and so involves the study of different methods of expression in sound. These methods may be more clearly defined as forms and styles. Forms are the ways in which at different periods music is cast into intelligible shapes. The fundamental principles remain constant: balance, proportion, repetition, contrast, variation, and so on. It is the detailed application of these principles that changes. Styles are the ways in which individuality, or it may be the general feeling of a period, finds expression. Hence we are conscious of music as a language with changes both in time and in place (in the form of regional varieties or dialects). To these methods of expression we should add the purposes for which music is designed, such as dancing, recreation, the stage or the Church. A sixteenth-century Mass, for example, will illustrate a particular form, a particular style and a particular purpose.

A study of individual styles leads to a study of composers, and hence of the reaction of their lives on their music. The objection is sometimes heard that biography is irrelevant. Music, it is suggested, develops by its own laws. Whatever truth there may be in this suggestion, we can certainly not ignore the instruments through which music finds expression. The biography of an artist is a study in personality. We try to discover how far the man and the musician were one, and if there seems to be a wide disparity to find the reasons for it. To the psychologist the lives of some composers are particularly interesting: Tchaikovsky is an obvious example.

Other composers we find baffling for lack of sufficient information: we know very little about Purcell apart from the official record of his career. Biography goes further than the individual. It tries also to see him in his environment, to study the social and political conditions in which he grew up and worked. The domination of the Church in the Middle Ages, the acceptance of patronage in the eighteenth century, the influence of liberal ideas at the time of the French Revolution—all these are instances of environment which had an appreciable affect on composers and on their work. To understand the man we must understand the world in which he lived.

A composer like Beethoven is both a product of his time and a unique phenomenon. He profits from the work of his predecessors, but they do not merely "pave the way" for him. The view once held that Haydn and Mozart were less important than Beethoven is ridiculous. And there is an equal danger in the view that Palestrina, because of the smoothness and technical perfection of his style, was the greatest composer of the so-called "polyphonic" period. In general we need to beware of the assumption that composition is an ineffectual struggle to do what later men do better.

It is the business of a historian to be critical, and this is as true of the history of music as of history in general. It is not sufficient for him to record facts: he must also judge their relative importance. In the case of music this involves a judgement of values—a judgement based not on an ordinary, everyday familiarity with music but on a close study of the styles of different periods. This opinion of the historian's function is not universally held. It is often maintained that appreciation of the values of music is irrelevant, and that the historian should record good and bad impartially, assessing changes of style rather than the merits of individual works or individual composers. If this principle, however, were faith-

fully observed, histories of music would be arid deserts of
scientific record, and the reader would be hard put to it to
understand why the music of the past should be studied at
all if its impact on our emotions is negligible. It is true that
the interpretation of canons of beauty changes from one age
to another, but they themselves remain immutable. If we
are seeking a guide to the riches of the past, we need someone
in whom they have stirred enthusiasm. The exaggerations
to which enthusiasm may lead are insignificant beside the
futility of an approach which refuses to recognize aesthetic
satisfaction as a spur to judgement.

The historian must also be constantly concerned with
the resources available at different periods. Without a
knowledge of these resources we may fail to understand what
composers were trying to do, and may judge them adversely
because they did not attempt what was inconceivable or
impossible. The history of musical instruments is not an
antiquarian pastime: it is indispensable to any clear realization of what the music of the past actually sounded like. Even
if the instruments themselves have not survived, descriptions
of them will often help us to get some idea of the principles of
colour and contrast which composers pursued. There is no
doubt that the whole of medieval music was intensely
concerned with colour. Only ignorance of the means used
for its performance could lead to the opinion that it was drab
and monotonous. Nor have we any right to assume that
resources different from ours were necessarily inadequate.
Art flourishes on limitations, and limitations are inseparable
from musical instruments of any period. There are always
notes that lie outside the compass of an instrument, there are
always passages which are impossible or so awkward as
to be totally ineffective. The practised composer knows how
to profit by these limitations and turn them to the best
advantage. When Haydn and Mozart were alive, the horn
with valves had not been invented and they were compelled

to use an instrument on which only a limited number of notes were available. But this does not mean that the "natural" horn was for them inadequate. It would have been inadequate for Wagner, but only because he took the existence of the valve-horn for granted and wrote in a style suggested by its potentialities.

We know that wood-wind playing was not always adequate in the eighteenth century: improvements in mechanism introduced in the nineteenth century made it easier to play in tune. But this is a matter which affects performance, not composition; and in fact present-day performers who have taken the trouble to master eighteenth-century wood-wind instruments have shown conclusively that they were capable not only of exact intonation but also of the most refined artistic expression. We are inclined also to suppose that virtuosity is a product of the last hundred years, whereas it has always been an important element in performance, particularly in the performance of solo music. The demands made on performers change from one century to another, and the achievements of an outstanding virtuoso in one age often become the common property of students in the next. But there still remains a great deal of brilliant music written by composers of the past which taxes very severely the abilities of modern performers, simply because the technique demanded does not form part of their normal equipment. Elizabethan virginal music is full of exasperating difficulties, and there can hardly be more than two or three players in the world who can perform Bach's trumpet parts on the instrument for which they were designed.

In general the historian of music has the same responsibilities as the political, the economic or the social historian. Like them he must treat events in an orderly sequence. He will show, for instance, how Beethoven's symphonies developed out of instrumental music of the mid-eighteenth century which was designed simply to entertain and amuse.

He will show how seventeenth-century opera turned more and more from declamation to song, and how the chromaticism of early twentieth-century music arose naturally from works like *Tristan und Isolde* and *Parsifal*. He too must refrain from imposing patterns. The history of music has not escaped the tendency to view the past as a series of cycles, nor the errors that arise from inventing analogies with the other arts. The absurdities to which such pattern-making can lead can be studied in Cecil Gray's *Predicaments* (see p. 56). Even the treatment of musical history as a series of periods, though convenient for examination purposes, may very well be misleading, particularly if it obscures the continuous development of the art. Causes and results will demand attention, no less than in history in general. We shall want to know how the Civil War in seventeenth-century England affected the course of English music, how Handel came to reside in England and become a national figure, how Grieg, instead of remaining a mere by-product of the Leipzig school, developed into a characteristically Norwegian composer.

To stimulate the reader's interest the historian of music needs not only style, without which his book will be unreadable, but also the ability to select musical examples which will illustrate as convincingly as possible the points which he is trying to emphasize. In the selection of these examples he must face a severe responsibility, since an example which is not truly representative may leave the reader with an entirely false idea of a composer or a style. To decide what is a pertinent illustration demands a very wide experience of music and an awareness of the limitations of the printed page. It also involves a finely tempered aesthetic judgement, since no one is likely to be impressed or stimulated by music which is weak or worthless. An example which is merely "interesting" is very often of no interest to anyone. All this means that the history of music is a very personal affair. This is true even of "omnibus" histories, to which several authorities have contributed, since each contributor will have his own personal approach. Whether a one-man history is better or worse than an omnibus one depends a great deal on its author. No doubt the field is so vast that one man cannot hope to have first-hand knowledge of it; and it is equally true that the expert knowledge contained in an omnibus history makes a work of this kind invaluable to the discriminating student. At the same time a single author of outstanding gifts brings to his work a unifying personality which cannot exist in a series of chapters by experts, and this may very well compensate for the lack of first-hand knowledge of this period or that. He may, in fact, be able to see the wood better for not having his attention so closely focused on the trees. Personality may even offer a stronger claim to survival than accuracy. No one now considers Burney to be reliable; but we still read him with a great deal of pleasure.

[1] Alfred Einstein, *Greatness in Music* (New York, 1941), pp. 197 foll.

CHAPTER II

THE SOURCES

THE sources for a history of music may be conveniently
classified under four heads: (1) the music itself, the study of
which involves not only a good deal of historical insight but
also a knowledge of palaeography and an expert understanding of symbols and conventions which are now obsolete;
(2) contemporary accounts of composers and musical
activities, autobiographies (e.g. those of Dittersdorf,
Spohr and Berlioz), letters (e.g. those of Mozart and Beethoven), and any other literature which throws incidental
light on the conditions and standards of performance; (3)
critical essays by contemporary writers (e.g. Schumann) and
treatises on the theory and practice of music (e.g. Praetorius's
Syntagma Musicum, which gives us detailed information
about instruments and instrumental performance in the early
seventeenth century); and finally (4) historical documents
in the strict sense of the term, i.e. records of official appointments and of payments made to musicians, entries in church
registers, programmes of concerts and operas, and so on.

We may consider first the music, whether manuscript or
printed. If it is earlier than 1500 it will be entirely manuscript, apart from a number of fifteenth-century missals.
Music-printing virtually began with Ottaviano dei Petrucci
(1466–1539), to whose pioneer activity we owe the publication
of many collections of secular part-songs, church music, lute
songs and lute solos. These editions, so far from being
primitive or clumsy, are still admired as models of fine
craftsmanship. Petrucci's example was followed by other
publishers in France, Germany, England and Spain: but it

was a long time before the printing of music became as
common as the printing of books. Most of the English church
music of the sixteenth and seventeenth centuries, for
example, survives only in manuscript; hundreds of operas
were never printed at all; and Bach's Passions and practically
all his cantatas remained in manuscript at his death. Later
composers did not fare much better. C. B. Oldman points
out that "of the six to seven hundred works by Mozart which
are recorded in Köchel's catalogue not more than seventy or
so were published during the composer's lifetime".[1] Schubert
wrote some 600 songs, but of these only 187 were printed
while he was alive: none of his symphonies appeared in print,
only three of his piano sonatas, and of his chamber music
only one string quartet and one piano trio.

The reasons for this are simple. Publishing has always
been governed largely by the laws of supply and demand.
Music-printing was a costly process, and no one in the ordinary way was likely to undertake it unless there was a prospect
of a reasonable return. Madrigals were printed in England
because there were a sufficient number of people to buy them.
Church music remained in manuscript (with one or two
exceptions) because there was less demand for it. Cathedral
organists were generally composers themselves and could
provide a substantial repertory; when they wanted the works
of other composers it was simple to acquire manuscript
copies. A move towards providing a printed repertory of
church music was made by John Barnard in 1641; but the
Civil War cut short the immediate development of the plan.
It was not until the eighteenth century that collections of
printed music for use in English cathedrals began to become
generally available. On the Continent a certain number of
large-scale works, both sacred and secular, appeared in
sumptuous editions; but these were generally due to the
munificence of a patron, who sought to acquire glory by
advertising his patronage.

Methods of notation have varied considerably. The earliest way of writing music for two or more voices or instruments was to set out the parts vertically one above the other—in score, as we should say. This lasted till the early thirteenth century. To us it seems a natural and obvious method. It was, in fact, very suitable for music in which all the parts had roughly the same number of notes and moved mostly together. But it was uneconomical if one part had nothing but a few long notes, while another had a number of short ones. A good deal of parchment could be saved by writing out the individual parts separately on the same page, or on opposite pages. They could then be read by a group of singers standing in front of a lectern. Such a method was not so suitable, however, for sociable music, where singers and instrumentalists wanted to be at ease. Hence the practice which begins to appear in the late fifteenth century of writing each part in a separate book, which a man can have in front of him on the table, without the trouble of looking over his neighbour. The *Glogauer Liederbuch*, a fifteenth-century collection of German part-songs and dances, is an example of this new practice, which proved so successful that it was widely adopted in the sixteenth century and became the normal method of printing music for vocal and instrumental ensembles.

The publication of scores, in the modern sense, dates from the late sixteenth century. The earliest cited example is a collection of four-part madrigals by Cipriano de Rore (1577), which bears the following title: "Tutti i Madrigali di Cipriano di Rore a quattro voci, spartiti et accommodati per sonar d'ogni sorte d'Instrumento perfetto, & per Qualunque studioso di Contrapunti" (All the four-part madrigals of Cipriano de Rore, barred and arranged for playing on any kind of "complete" instrument and for students of counterpoint). This is clearly an exceptional publication: it has a double purpose—to facilitate performance of the madrigals on a "complete" instrument (i.e. one capable of playing all the parts, such as harpsichord or organ) and to enable students to study the part-writing. The verb *spartire* (or *partire*) means "to bar" (hence the Italian *partitura*, the German *Partitur*, and the French *partition*, all of which mean a score). Bar-lines were not necessary in separate part-books, since the note-values were accurately represented in each part and needed only to be observed; but in a score the drawing of vertical lines at intervals was necessary as a guide to the eye and to avoid confusion, particularly if there were different rhythms in the different parts. It was the growth of the orchestra in seventeenth-century opera which made the provision of a score something more than an occasional curiosity: the more performers there were taking part, the more it became necessary for the person directing the performance to see what was supposed to be happening. Our modern orchestral practice retains the innovation of the seventeenth century and also the older tradition of the sixteenth century: the conductor has a score, and the players have separate parts.

The history of the signs employed for individual notes, or for groups of notes, is more complex. In their earliest form, adapted from the Greek accents, they indicated merely the rise and fall of a melody, with no precise indication of pitch and no indication of rhythm. These so-called "neumes" were therefore hardly notation at all in our sense of the word: they were useless for anyone who had not already heard the melody sung. But they served well enough the purpose of transmitting the oral tradition of Gregorian chant under the direction of a choirmaster. No doubt it was the occasional lack of a direct contact with this tradition which led to the practice, in use by the eleventh century, of distinguishing carefully the relative height of the neumes. Before long the scribe's task was facilitated by a horizontal line, similar to that used for writing the words. This was so obvious a convenience that other lines were added. The modern staff, in regular use by the twelfth century, was thus the product of necessity. At the same time the neumes, now carefully placed on lines or spaces, were modified in shape. The single notes shrank into dots or squares, and the combinations of two or more notes acquired conventional forms related to the shapes of the single notes. The exact definition of rhythm was a later stage. This, too, was a product of necessity. The development of polyphony in the thirteenth century made it increasingly difficult for singers to co-ordinate their parts without guidance; and hence the practice of giving a rhythmical interpretation to an ambiguous notation gave place to an actual distinction between note-values and a difference in the shapes assigned to them.

We need only summarize subsequent developments. The fourteenth century saw the creation of signs necessary to give precision to smaller note-values, and in the latter half of the fifteenth century, for reasons of economy and clarity, the principal note-values came to be written in outline only (like our semibreve and minim), black notes being reserved for crotchets and smaller values. Throughout this time the old combinations of two, three or more notes (the "ligatures") survived, as did the traditional rules for their interpretation. On all these matters, and on the understanding of a very complicated system of time-signatures, the theorists throw considerable light. They do not always agree with each other, and their writings do not by any means solve all the problems that confront a modern editor. But without them we should flounder helplessly in any attempt at transcription and would only be able to reach a probable solution by an uncertain use of trial and error. The sixteenth century inherited the old traditions; but much that was complex and ambiguous in them came to be discarded. By about 1600 a system of notation had been achieved which was reasonably simple and precise, and which in all essentials is the same as ours.

Staff notation is in origin a notation for singers, though it came to be used eventually for every kind of instrument. It shows the rise and fall of a melody and so corresponds to a singer's reactions. In the early Middle Ages other systems were also tried, among them the use of letters to designate the notes. Letters, however, do not suggest a vocal pattern, and hence this type of notation could not compete with the obvious advantages of the staff. But since it had the advantage of indicating the pitch precisely it was used for keyboard music in the fourteenth and fifteenth centuries, with the addition of signs to indicate the correct octave and metrical symbols to indicate the rhythm. At the same time there was no obvious reason why keyboard music should not be written on two staves, one for the right hand and the other for the left, and this began to become the general practice in the early sixteenth century. The letter notation, to which even Bach resorted in the early eighteenth century when hard pressed for space, was known as "tablature". A wholly different kind of tablature was used for the lute and similar instruments. This was not a universal notation, applicable to any medium, but a system of instructions to performers. Letters or figures indicated where the fingers were to stop the strings, the strings themselves being indicated by horizontal lines. Though of limited application and designed primarily for the benefit of performers, this was a precise notation and, like the keyboard tablatures, had the advantage of distinguishing B♮ from B♭, F♮ from F♯ and so on.

Though the conventions of staff notation had been simplified by the seventeenth century and remained reasonably stable, we still have the problem of interpretation.[2] The practice of using figured bass, which dates roughly from the beginning of this period, was a great practical convenience and saved composers a great deal of time. But it is by no means an easy matter, even with the aid of theoretical writers, to recapture the traditions of its performance. The performance of ornaments, whether written or implied, also creates problems to which there is no one simple solution. Add to this the alterations of rhythm which were conventional in the seventeenth and early eighteenth centuries (though not indicated in the notation), the frequent absence of any signs of dynamics, speed or expression, and the uncertainty of the bowing of string parts, and it becomes obvious that there are many obstacles to be faced before we can even begin to pretend to an understanding of the music of the past. The same gulf does not separate us from the music of the late nineteenth century. By that time indications of expression and tempo had become profuse, and the metronome was an accurate guide to speed. More than this, we are near enough to the period to have something like an authentic tradition of interpretation. But before long that tradition will become obscure and unreliable, and we shall be in much the same position as we are with regard to earlier music, uncertain whether traditions are genuine or of recent growth. These doubts will hardly arise in the future when historians come to describe the music of the twentieth century. Gramophone records, often performed or conducted by the composers, will supply a new and more exact kind of evidence.

Every honest historian would like to be able to work entirely from original sources; but the labour would be impossibly vast. Like the student and the music-lover he is compelled to depend to a large extent on modern editions. The idea of providing such editions is comparatively recent. Up to the latter part of the eighteenth century musicians were primarily interested in the music of their own time. The only notable exception was the Church, where many pieces of old music continued to be performed on account of their fitness for an unchanging liturgy. But towards the end of the eighteenth century there was a growing awareness that a great deal of valuable music of the past lay buried in libraries, and the popularity of Handel's works after his death suggested that music had a life of its own beyond the frontiers of the grave. That popularity encouraged Samuel Arnold to attempt a large-scale edition of Handel (1786), which though incomplete and inaccurate was a remarkable piece of pioneering in a new field. Attempts were also made at complete editions of Mozart (1798) and Haydn (1800). The problems to be solved, however, demanded a more thorough scholarship. The inauguration of the Bach-Gesellschaft in 1850 set a new standard of accuracy and completeness. Nine years later Friedrich Chrysander embarked single-handed on a new edition of Handel—a gigantic labour which only the greatest tenacity could have achieved. These two editions— of Bach and Handel—have remained standard works down to the present day, in spite of the fact that in detail they inevitably need modification.[3] Their example led to the publication of complete editions of many other composers— among them Beethoven, Mendelssohn, Palestrina, Mozart, Chopin, Schumann, Schubert, Schütz, Sweelinck, Victoria, Brahms and Praetorius. In some cases projected editions have remained incomplete, generally for lack of financial support: this is true of the editions of Lassus and Buxtehude. The edition of Haydn begun earlier in this century also came to an untimely end. It has now been replaced by an entirely new edition, which is still in course of publication.

The publication of these complete editions drew attention to a mass of music by other composers, known or anonymous, who deserved recognition. A series of volumes devoted either to single works by particular composers or to selections from the works of several was inaugurated by Robert Eitner in 1869 under the title *Publikationen älterer praktischer und theoretischer Musikwerke*. A similar collection of more limited scope—*L'arte musicale in Italia*—was begun by Luigi Torchi in 1897. Other series of a similar kind have from time to time been produced by individual editors. But the most substantial contribution has been made by societies. The

German, Austrian and Bavarian series of *Denkmäler* (Monuments) have made available a vast amount of music by composers who were natives of those countries or active in them. The Austrian series, for example, includes all that survives of Cesti's opera *Il pomo d'oro* (1667) and the original Italian version of Gluck's *Orfeo*. It is impossible to enumerate here all the other series which have appeared in the present century in France, Germany, Italy, Spain and elsewhere. A convenient list for quick reference will be found in Willi Apel's *Harvard Dictionary of Music* under the heading "Editions, Historical", and on a more elaborate scale in the German encyclopedia *Die Musik in Geschichte und Gegenwart* under the heading "Denkmäler". A brief mention, however, should be made here of the contribution made by English scholars—notably the publications of the Plainsong and Mediaeval Music Society, the series *Tudor Church Music*, the editions of the English madrigalists and lutenist composers by E. H. Fellowes, and more recently *Musica Britannica*, published by the Royal Musical Association, which includes the complete works of Dunstable.

The value of all these editions is in proportion to their reliability. The methods employed by the editors are of minor importance provided the results can be trusted. The older editors, for example, were generally at pains to reproduce the original clefs and note-values, whereas the modern tendency is to reduce the number of clefs to those in everyday use and to use the crotchet as the standard note-value in place of the minim, semibreve, or even breve of earlier usage. Any form of simplification which makes the music immediately accessible to the greatest number of people is obviously desirable, since there is no virtue in obscurity. But whatever form simplification of notation may take, it is still nothing but a matter of practical convenience: it neither ensures nor precludes accuracy. There are many varieties of editing, but there is only one basic method which inspires confidence, and that is the clear and unmistakable distinction between what is in the original and what has been supplied or emended by the editor. Whether the editor prints the original text and adds an emendation in a footnote, or emends the text and explains what he has done, is immaterial, provided the reader can be certain that nothing has been changed without some indication of the fact.

Even so there will often be cases where it is desirable to check the transcription from the original. In some cases this is possible by referring to a photographic facsimile. One of the earliest of such facsimiles was the reproduction of Handel's autograph of *Messiah*, published in 1868. Unfortunately this is largely useless for reference, since the reproduction is very clumsily executed and the result is not a true facsimile. Later publications of this kind have been more scrupulous. They include the volume of *Early Bodleian Music* published by Sir John Stainer, the first edition of Monteverdi's *Orfeo*, the manuscripts of Bach's *Mass in B minor* and the *St. Matthew Passion*, several collections of troubadour and trouvère songs and a number of other important medieval manuscripts. Where published facsimiles are not available one must have recourse to photostats specially ordered or to microfilms. The invention of microfilms has revolutionized the process of becoming acquainted with original sources. They are not only cheap to acquire but can also be stored in a very small space. The laborious journeys which scholars were once forced to undertake have not become entirely superfluous, since nothing can properly take the place of an original; but for most ordinary purposes microfilms enable the student to command the resources of libraries in widely distant parts of the world without stirring from his study.

Information about modern editions can be acquired only by experience. In addition to the two works of reference mentioned above, the biographical entries in standard dictionaries of music should supply a large number of references, and these can be confirmed or supplemented by up-to-date historical works, such as Gustave Reese's *Music in the Middle Ages* and *Music in the Renaissance* or Manfred Bukofzer's *Music in the Baroque Era*, which have thorough bibliographies. Inevitably such references rapidly become incomplete, since so much new material appears every year. Particulars of additional material can, however, be found in periodicals which provide lists of new publications, such as *Acta Musicologica*. Information about the original sources on which modern editions are based is best obtained from the editions themselves, but it may often need to be amplified by consulting the numerous catalogues of printed and manu-script music in the great public libraries and in smaller collections such as Christ Church, Oxford. For those who have neither time nor the opportunity to consult complete or substantial editions anthologies such as the Harvard *Historical Anthology* or Arnold Schering's *Geschichte der Musik in Beispielen* can serve a very useful purpose. They remain, however, selections from a vast mass of material, and the student is here as much dependent on the editor's choice as he is when studying the examples in a history.

The twentieth century has brought a further aid to the study of the music of the past—the gramophone record. It would be a mistake to suppose that the older historians were necessarily indifferent to the value of hearing the music of which they wrote. Fétis in Paris was a pioneer in the organiza-tion of historical concerts in the nineteenth century, and Ouseley in Oxford illustrated his lectures by carefully chosen examples of sixteenth-century works. But enterprise of this kind could not supply what the student urgently needs—the opportunity of hearing old music constantly and in his own time. Anthologies of gramophone records are open to the same objection as anthologies of musical examples; there is also the further objection that many details of interpretation are likely to be open to dispute. But these objections are of minor importance beside the value of realizing that music of all periods is a living art which belongs not to the printed page but to the world of sound. A single record can do more to stimulate imagination than half a dozen pages of description. The student who is able to use, for example, the French series entitled *Anthologie sonore* or the H.M.V. *History of Music in Sound* will find, after the initial strangeness of unfamiliar idioms has worn off, that the music of the past has become a vivid, intimate experience. Familiar terms such as motet, madrigal, baroque opera and cantata will have acquired a new meaning. It is rather like meeting face to face a person whom one has hitherto known only by correspondence.

We come now to our second group of sources. Contemporary accounts of musical activities are rare before the eighteenth century. Until then we depend largely on isolated references in works not specifically devoted to music. A good deal of information about medieval practice, for instance, can be derived from incidental passages in poetry or prose which happen to mention instruments or methods of performance; and the composite picture which they present can be confirmed by illustrations in manuscripts and representations in sculpture.[4] So also with later periods. Books like Castiglione's *Libro del cortegiano* (Book of the Courtier) in the early sixteenth century and Peacham's *Compleat Gentleman* a century later give us a vivid idea of the part that music might be expected to play in the life of the leisured classes. Shakespeare's plays are full of allusions to music which illuminate the Elizabethan scene,[5] and Pepys's diary provides us with a first-hand account of many details of musical life in Restoration England. The letters of Saint-Évremond and Madame de Sévigné perform a similar service for the court of Louis XIV, and a little later the pages of the *Spectator* and the *Tatler* tell us much about musical conditions, and musical prejudices, in the England of Queen Anne.

Here are some examples of the kind of information to be derived from these sources. In the thirteenth-century *Roman de la Rose* there is a description of a person carrying a portative organ,

> Où il-meisme souffle et touche
> Et chante avec, à pleine bouche,
> Motès o trèble et teneure,

which not only tells us that motets could be sung by a solo voice with instrumental accompaniment but also furnishes a precise parallel to the many miniatures which represent performers on this instrument. Here, long before the sixteenth-century lute song, is a picture of a singer supplying his own accompaniment, undeterred by the double labour of working the hand-bellows of the organ and playing it at the same time. In the fourteenth century Giovanni da Prato's *Il paradiso degli Alberti* (1389) gives a lively idea of the cultured life of Florence in his day, telling us how a select audience were moved by the superlative beauty of love-songs performed by the blind organist Francesco Landini.[6] Similarly in the fifteenth century Martin le Franc's poem *Le Champion des Dames* (about 1440) praises Dufay and Binchois for the pleasure which their music affords with its "frisque concordance", mentioning incidentally that they adopted the English style and followed Dunstable. Passages of this kind have a particular value in confirming what any sensible person would assume to be true—that at all periods music has been valued for the emotional satisfaction which it affords to listeners and for the stimulus which it offers to the imagination. If we find that the music of remote ages makes no immediate appeal to us, the fault lies not in the music but in the distance of time which separates us from it. One of the obvious ends of historical study is to narrow that gap.

Sometimes our sources supply a useful corrective to any rash generalization about the universal appreciation of music. Castiglione's *Il Cortegiano* (1528), for example, has an illuminating passage about a soldier who had no use for dancing or music and was rebuked by a lady in these terms:

> I should think that as you are not at the war, nor in any likelihood of fighting, it would be a good thing if you were to have yourself thoroughly well oiled and put away in a cupboard with all your fighting gear until you were wanted, so as not to get more rusty than you are already.[7]

The interest of this story is not so much in the fact that music was held in high regard by people of culture but in the evidence that there were those to whom it meant nothing at all. If we turn to the seventeenth century we find also that opera, in spite of its rapid conquest of Europe, did not meet with universal acceptance. Saint-Évremond confessed that opera bored him: the music might be delightful and the spectacle charming, but the plots and the librettos were generally contemptible. Addison in the *Spectator* reveals a similar antipathy to opera as performed in England in the early eighteenth century.

Biographies of musicians were non-existent before the late eighteenth century, possibly because musicians were not considered important enough to justify this attention. An early example is Mainwaring's *Memoirs of the Life of the Late George Frederic Handel* (1760), published a year after Handel's death. It is inaccurate in detail but gives some idea of the immense esteem in which Handel was held in England. It was followed in 1802 by the first biography of Bach, written by Johann Nicolaus Forkel and published at a time when Bach's works had been very largely forgotten. Evidence for the lives of earlier composers, apart from letters and historical documents, often has to be extracted from prefaces to their publications or from incidental references in contemporary works, and these materials naturally continue to be the source for later biographies. John Dowland, in the address to the reader printed in his *First Booke of Songs or Ayres* (1597), tells us how widely he had travelled on the Continent—in France, Germany, and Italy, where, he hints, he enjoyed a great reputation. He also mentions that he had the friendliest association with Luca Marenzio. These facts would not otherwise have been known, and they are an important contribution to our knowledge of the composer. In particular they suggest a critical examination of his music to see what traces there may be of Continental influence and which countries impressed him most.

Incidental references, however brief, are often illuminating. J. G. Ziegler in 1746 tells us something of Bach's teaching:

> As concerns the playing of chorales, I was instructed by my teacher, Capellmeister Bach, who is still living, not to play the songs merely offhand but according to the sense (*Affect*) of the words.[8]

On Beethoven we are particularly well informed. Many of his pupils, friends and chance acquaintances have left us accounts of his behaviour and his practical musicianship. We owe to his pupil Ries an account of an incident when Beethoven, angry with a waiter who had mistaken his order, flung the dish at the man's head and then, as the gravy poured down the culprit's face, hurled insults at him.[9] Here to the life is the tempestuous Beethoven as we know him from many of his Allegros. Another pupil, Czerny, has left us an excellent account of Beethoven's piano-playing and the details of his instruction:

> Nobody equalled him in the rapidity of his scales, double

trills, skips, etc.—not even Hummel. His bearing while playing
was masterfully quiet, noble and beautiful . . . his fingers were
very powerful, not long, and broadened at the tips by much
playing. . . . In teaching he laid great stress on a correct position of
the fingers (after the school of Emanuel Bach, which he used in
teaching me); he could scarcely span a tenth. He made frequent
use of the pedals, much more frequent than is indicated in his
works.[10]

A very large number of letters from composers survive.
These frequently throw light on the conditions of the time
and on the individual's reaction to his environment; but they
are particularly valuable when they include a discussion of the
principles of composition or the methods employed in a
particular work. Among the most vivid letters are those of
Mozart and Busoni, both of whom had the gift of photograph-
ing a scene or an incident and recording it on paper. The more
ancient the letters, the more significant is the contribution
which they can make to our knowledge of a period. We are
particularly fortunate in having so many of Monteverdi's.[11]
In them we can not only study the background to the new art
of opera in the seventeenth century but also learn something
of the psychology of the composer. In a well-known letter,
dating from 1616, he discusses the proposal that he should
write music for the winds in the opera *Le Nozze di Tetide*.
How, he asks, is this possible? Orpheus, he recalls, stirred the
emotions because he was a man, and Ariadne because she was
a woman. The brief reference to two of his most famous
operas gives us in a nutshell the secret of his success. To him
the characters in opera were not lay figures but human beings;
and it is as human beings that they emerge in performance.

One of the most illuminating of Mozart's letters is the one
in which he discusses the details of his opera *Die Entführung*.[12] We learn from it his views on the function of
music as an expression of dramatic emotion and on the
limits to what is permissible:

Passions, whether violent or not, must never be expressed in such a way as to excite disgust, and . . . music, even in the most terrible situations, must never offend the ear.

We learn too of his relations with his librettist, and of the impatience which led him to write the music of an aria before he had even told the librettist what words he wanted. We find a rather similar situation in a letter written to Hugo von Hofmannsthal by Richard Strauss on the subject of *Der Rosenkavalier*.[13] He outlines an addition which he wants to the scene for Baron Ochs in Act I, and remarks:

Would you add some more text here: the music is all ready and I only need the words for accompaniment and filling in?

Autobiography as a source is apt to be less reliable, largely because composers who write about themselves seem often to be self-conscious or to yield to the temptation to dramatize their achievements. Dittersdorf's account of his dealings with the orchestra of the Bishop of Grosswardein[14] leave us in no doubt about his opinion of himself as a *Kapellmeister*; but it would have been interesting, none the less, to have the orchestra's views on Dittersdorf. No composer was more inclined to uncertain reminiscence (to give it no harsher name) than Berlioz. His account of the first performance of his *Requiem* is well known.[15] It alleges that Habeneck, who was conducting, neglected his duties at a critical moment and took snuff, and the situation was saved, it seems, only by the intervention of the composer. There are serious reasons, however, for doubting the complete accuracy of this story,[16] and the manner in which it is told seems to glorify to excess the author's part in the proceedings. More agreeable, though less highly coloured, are the amiable recollections of Spohr, who has left us, among other things, a telling pen-portrait of John Field, a "pale, overgrown youth". whom he met in St. Petersburg and the "dreamy melancholy" of whose playing

he much admired.[17] And sometimes we can glean interesting
information about great men from the autobiographies of less
distinguished musicians. The Irish tenor Michael Kelly was
full of his own importance; but his first-hand descriptions of
the first performance of *Figaro* and his intimate account of
its composer deserve a place in any but the most superficial
biography of Mozart.[18]

More valuable in general than sources of this kind are
considered accounts of contemporary music by skilled
observers. Outstanding among eighteenth-century works of
this kind are the two accounts which Burney wrote of his
travels on the Continent to collect materials for his history
of music.[19] We may smile at the philosophy of music which
he outlines in his introduction, particularly at his answer to
the question "What is the use of music?":

It is easy to point out the humane and important purposes to
which it has been applied. Its assistance has been called in by the
most respectable profession in this kingdom, in order to open the
purses of the affluent for the support of the distressed offspring
of their deceased brethren.[20]

But we could hardly dispense with the vivid account of
his visit to Carl Philipp Emanuel Bach, who

not only played, but looked like one inspired. His eyes were fixed,
his under lip fell, and drops of effervescence distilled from his
countenance,[21]

or the description of one of the conservatories at Naples,
where the boys were practising all sorts of vocal and instrumental music in a single room:

The jumbling them all together in this manner may be
convenient for the house, and may teach the boys to attend to
their own parts with firmness, whatever else may be going forward

at the same time; it may likewise give them force, by obliging them to play loud in order to hear themselves; but in the midst of such jargon, and continued dissonance, it is wholly impossible to give any kind of polish or finishing to their performance; hence the slovenly coarseness so remarkable in their public exhibitions; and the total want of taste, neatness, and expression in all these young musicians, till they have acquired them elsewhere.[22]

Our third general category of sources consists of criticism, essays and treatises on music. Criticism in the modern sense can hardly be said to exist before the eighteenth century. Earlier literature on music consists mainly, though not exclusively, of technical treatises. A whole series of theoretical works by writers of the Middle Ages have survived. Some of these were printed by Martin Gerbert, Abbot of St. Blaise in the Black Forest, in 1784,[23] and a further collection by Edmond de Coussemaker from 1864–76.[24] One or two have been published more recently in modern editions, but critical texts are few, and little has so far been done to rectify the numerous errors to be found in Coussemaker's edition. The subject-matter of these treatises is principally church music, since education was in the hands of churchmen. They include detailed rules for musical notation and hence are useful guides to the transcription of medieval music, though they are not necessarily evidence of contemporary practice. Thus the ninth-century treatise *Musica enchiriadis*, formerly attributed to Hucbald, describes both strict and free *organum* —the first consisting of continuous parallel fourths and fifths between the parts, the second including other intervals; but there is no reason to suppose that the first is earlier historically than the second, or indeed that either was the normal way of writing music at the time the treatise was written. In general one finds that theorists tend to codify the practice of the past rather than to explain the methods of their contemporaries. An exception to the general run of

medieval theorists is Johannes de Grocheo,[25] who appears to
have been a lecturer in Paris about 1300. In addition to dis-
cussing church music, like the other theorists, he also offers
some very interesting information about secular song, including the *chanson de geste*. The obscurities which not infrequently appear in the treatises of this period are probably due to the
fact that some at least of them seem to survive in the form of
lecture notes—a form which has never at any period been a
guarantee of accuracy.

Among the difficulties which confront the modern student
of medieval treatises is the fact that technical terms do not
always seem to be used in exactly the same sense, or alternatively that more than one term is used for the same thing.
The first systematic attempt to codify terminology was made
by Johannes Tinctoris in the fifteenth century. His
Terminorum musicae diffinitorium (Dictionary of musical
terms) dates from about 1474.[26] Another work by Tinctoris,
entitled *Proportionale musices*, offers an example of the incidental mention of actual composers which, however rarely
it occurs, is one of the most valuable features of theoretical
writings. It is here that we find the famous definition of later
fifteenth-century music as a new art, whose "fount and origin
is said to have been among the English", with the additional
information that Dunstable was the most considerable English
composer—a passage which confirms the reference by Martin
le Franc quoted on p. 32.

Tradition was powerful in the world of theory. We find
that writers of the sixteenth century were still faithful to the
past. Glareanus, in his *Dodekachordon* (1547) maintains that
there are twelve modes, parallel to those of Greek music,
at a time when the influence of the church modes had
already been undermined. Similarly Morley's *Plaine and
Easie Introduction to Practicall Musicke* (1597)[27] includes
much that was out of date by the time it was published. Yet
both these works are valuable, Glareanus for his enlightened

criticism of early sixteenth-century composers, Morley for his comments on various musical forms and methods of composition—for example, the motet:

A Motet is properlie a song made for the church, either upon some hymne or Antheme, or such like, and that name I take to have beene given to that kinde of musicke in opposition to the other which they called *Canto fermo*, and we do commonlie call plainsong, for as nothing is more opposit to standing and firmnes then [i.e. than] motion, so did they give the Motet that name of moving, because it is in a manner quight contrarie to the other, which after some sort, and in respect of the other standeth still. This kind of al others which are made on a ditty [i.e. with words], requireth most art, and moveth and causeth most strange effects in the hearer, being aptlie framed for the dittie and well expressed by the singer, for it will draw the auditor (and speciallie the skilfull auditor) into a devout and reverent kind of consideration of him for whose praise it was made. [28]

The value of this comment is not impaired by the fact that the etymology proposed for the word is wildly inaccurate.

In spite of its fidelity to the past sixteenth-century theory is more liberal in its outlook, being concerned also with music as a form of expression and with the practical means of performance. Martin Agricola's *Musica instrumentalis deudsch* (1529)[29] was a pioneer work in the description of musical instruments—a task that was continued in more detail and with more precision by Michael Praetorius in his *Syntagma Musicum* (1615–19),[30] which deals also with various forms of musical composition. We find also a number of books giving instruction in the playing of instruments: several lute tutors were published in the sixteenth century—an indication of the vogue which the instrument enjoyed among amateurs. In England the popularity of the bass viol as a solo instrument led to the publication of Christopher Simpson's *The Division-Violist* (1659). The seventeenth century even produced a tutor for the trumpet—Girolamo Fantini's *Modo per imparare a sonare di tromba* (1638).[31] The new technique of figured bass which played such an important part in the early operas also called for instruction: the demand was answered by a slim manual by Agostino Agazzari, entitled *Del sonare sopra'l basso* (1607).[32]

In the eighteenth century instruction books for particular instruments often contain valuable information about methods of performance and the practice of ornamentation. Johann Joachim Quantz's *Versuch einer Anweisung die Flöte traversiere zu spielen* (1752)[33] is far more than a mere tutor for the flute: it embraces the whole art of interpretation. The same is true of Carl Philipp Emanuel Bach's *Versuch über die wahre Art das Clavier zu spielen* (1753).[34] By now the practice of playing from figured bass was 150 years old; but since it was a part of the necessary equipment of all musicians there was still room for the publication of new works on the subject.[35] It was natural that emphasis should have been laid on the bass in the teaching of harmony and composition. J. S. Bach, according to Forkel,[36]

did not begin with dry counterpoints that led nowhere, as was done by other teachers of music in his time. . . . He proceeded at once to the pure thorough bass in four parts, and insisted particularly on the writing out of these parts because thereby the idea of the pure progression of the harmony is rendered the most evident. He then proceeded to chorales. In the exercises, he at first set the basses himself and made the pupils invent only the alto and tenor to them. By degrees, he let them also make the basses.

As we get nearer to our own time theoretical writings naturally become of less importance for the history of music, partly because of the greater accessibility of the actual music and, more important, because of the survival of traditions of performance.

The earlier essayists on music, like the older theorists,

show an attachment to the past. Excellent examples are the *Memoirs of Musick* and *The Musicall Gramarian* left in manuscript by Roger North and printed in modern times.[37] The two essays are in fact different versions of the same theme, written about 1728 when the author was an old man. Both of them start with a discussion of music in the ancient world, about which North knew next to nothing. Such speculation about antiquity was natural in an inquiring age. Needless to say the value of such essays does not lie in these excursions into ancient history but in their references to contemporary history or to the recent past. North's memory of his younger days was by no means accurate; but his essays reproduce very effectively something of the temper of musical life in Restoration times, and his account of the first public concerts given in London is not surpassed by any other source.

In general the eighteenth century encouraged the philosophical and eventually the encyclopedic discussion of music. In Germany Johann Mattheson was a voluminous writer on music and also edited *Critica Musica* (1722–25), the first musical periodical. The duty of critics to criticize was well understood, and writers were not concerned with the judgement of posterity. Johann Adolph Scheibe, in his *Der critische Musicus* (1737), has some very severe remarks to make about a composer who is not named but who is known to be Bach from a spirited reply which was made by Johann Abraham Birnbaum. Scheibe praises Bach's skill as a performer but is critical of the style of his music. "This great man," he says,

would be the admiration of whole nations if he had more amenity, if he did not take away the natural element in his pieces by giving them a turgid and confused style, and if he did not darken their beauty by an excess of art.

The music, in short, is artificial:

One admires the onerous labour and uncommon effort—
which, however, are vainly employed, since they conflict with
Nature.[38]

Enlightened criticism at this period did much to set composers, and musicians in general, thinking about the nature
of their art. Long before Gluck's so-called "reforms" of
opera had taken practical shape Algarotti in his *Saggio
sopra l'opera in musica* (1755)[39] had drawn attention to the
absurdities of many of the operatic conventions of his day
and suggested remedies; and he was not alone in his criticism.
In France the publication of the *Encyclopédie*, the first volume
of which appeared in 1751, gave an opportunity to writers
not only to define terms but also to criticize their current
interpretation. In England Charles Avison of Newcastle
upon Tyne produced *An Essay on Musical Expression* (1752)
which is many ways ingenuous but is original in its insistence
on the individual characteristics of instruments and in its
suggestion that new music should be reviewed in periodicals.

In the nineteenth century the flood of literature swells into
full tide. We find many composers active as critics—Schumann, Liszt, Wagner and Berlioz are notable examples. The
reason for this is simple. Musicians were now drawn from a
wider circle. They were not merely the sons of professional
musicians following in their father's footsteps: they came
often from cultured families and were themselves men of
literary ability. At the same time a new race of professional
critics arose, of whom Hanslick in Vienna is the typical
example. The new middle-class public, keenly interested in
music, was eager to see it discussed in the newspapers and
reviews and to test its own reactions by the judgements of
experts. The composers were not necessarily the best
critics. They could err through over-enthusiasm or through
prejudice. Schumann's opinion of Sterndale Bennett seems in
retrospect hopelessly exaggerated. Writing of Bennett's third
piano concerto he confesses himself

astonished at the early dexterity of this artist-hand, the con-
nection of the whole, its reposeful arrangement, its euphonious
language, its purity of thought.

And he concludes:

Were there many artists like Sterndale Bennett, all fears for the
future progress of our art would be silenced.[40]

On the other hand Berlioz found himself quite unable to
understand the prelude to Wagner's *Tristan und Isolde*. He
could find in it

no other theme than a sort of chromatic moan, full of dissonant
chords, of which the long appoggiaturas that replace the real note
only increase the cruelty.[41]

Hugo Wolf's criticism of Brahms was inspired by more
than a lack of understanding: the evidence of malice is
unmistakable. He describes the D minor piano concerto
as "unhealthy stuff", and the violin concerto as "a most
disagreeable piece, full of platitudes". The fourth symphony
is marked by "nullity, emptiness and hypocrisy"; and his
notice of the third symphony exhausts the resources of
metaphor in the pursuit of venom.[42] Such criticism must
be read with a grain of salt; nor can it be properly understood
without a knowledge of Wolf's environment in Vienna and
some appreciation of his passionate enthusiasm for Wagner.
At the same time it must be recognized that there were others
who refused to bow the knee to Brahms. Even so impartial
and enlightened a critic as Bernard Shaw could write in
1888 that Brahms's music was "at bottom only a prodigiously
elaborated compound of incoherent reminiscences", though
nearly fifty years later he published a humble recantation.[43]
Shaw was undoubtedly the most brilliant of all English
critics, and one of the best informed. We may read him, if we

like, for the pleasure afforded by his wit and versatility; but there is also a solid documentary value in his published articles. They bring before us with striking clarity the state of English music at a time which is now remote to all but old men. This is true also of his excursions abroad. His description of Bayreuth deserves a place in any anthology of opera criticism: the steam in *Parsifal* "filled the house with a smell of laundry and melted axillary gutta-percha linings", "the much boasted staging" was "marred by obsolete contrivances which would astonish us at the Lyceum as much as a return to candle-lighting". And though the conditions for hearing the music were perfect, the performance did not "touch the excellence of one which Richter conducted at the Albert Hall".[44]

Documentary evidence, in the strict sense of the word, is perhaps the least interesting of the sources for musical history, but not the least important. It includes the records of appointments in royal and princely establishments, accounts of payments made to musicians, entries of birth and death in church registers, and the like. Such information is generally purely factual and non-committal. We learn, for example, from the Lord Chamberlain's records that Purcell left the Chapel Royal, when his voice broke in 1673, with the customary suit of clothes and a bursary of £30 a year.[45] We learn from Schubert's school reports that he was good in all his studies and was observed to have "a special musical talent".[46] We can study the pompous document in which Queen Elizabeth I granted a monopoly of music-printing to Thomas Tallis and William Byrd (see p. 93). Sometimes the information will be more colourful. The sober records of the English Chapel Royal are enlivened by the recital of an extraordinary incident which occurred in 1620, when one of the yeomen of the vestry, a man of singularly unpleasant habits, became violently drunk and assaulted Orlando Gibbons.[47] And the genius of Bach has by accident im-

mortalized the remark made by an obscure councillor of
Leipzig and preserved in the council's proceedings. The
occasion was the appointment of a cantor to St. Thomas's.
Graupner, from Darmstadt, was the favoured candidate, but
he could not obtain leave from his employer. In consequence,
said Councillor Plaz, "since the best man could not be
obtained, mediocre ones would have to be accepted".[48]
The mediocre musician who was in due course appointed was
Bach.

Documents of this kind may be described as the raw
materials of history. As a rule they need no musicianship for
their collection and can easily be assembled by anyone trained
in historical research. When collected, however, they often
have considerable importance for the historian of music.
They may help to complete a picture or provide a missing
link in a chain of evidence. Above all they help to establish a
reliable chronology of a composer's life. The interpretation of
such documents may very well require something more than
the accuracy of the trained researcher; and indeed there are
not infrequently occasions when musicianship is necessary
for their discovery, since only the musician may know where
to look and what to look for. It may very well be argued that
it is a waste of a musician's time to indulge in spade-work of
this kind; but in the long run the result is often a more complete collation of material and one more closely related to
other studies in the same field.

[1] Emily Andersoñ, *The Letters of Mozart and his Family* (London,
1938), vol. iii, p. 1453.
[2] For a fuller discussion of this question see Thurston Dart, *The
Interpretation of Music* (Hutchinson's University Library, London, 1954).
[3] New complete editions of Bach and Handel are in progress.
[4] For the latter see G. Kinsky, *A History of Music in Pictures* (London,
1930).
[5] See E. W. Naylor, *Shakespeare and Music*, 2nd ed. (London, 1931).
[6] See L. Ellinwood, *The Works of Francesco Landini* (Cambridge,
Mass., 1945), p. xv.
[7] Translation by Edward J. Dent in *The Oxford History of Music*,
introductory vol. (London, 1929), p. 215.

[8] Hans T. David and Arthur Mendel, *The Bach Reader*, 2nd ed. (New York, 1966), p. 237.

[9] *Beethoven: Impressions of Contemporaries* (New York, 1927), p. 58.

[10] A. W. Thayer, *The Life of Ludwig van Beethoven*, ed. Elliot Forbes (Princeton, 1964), p. 368.

[11] Printed in G. F. Malipiero, *Claudio Monteverdi* (Milan, 1929).

[12] Emily Anderson, *The Letters of Mozart and his Family*, 2nd ed. (London, 1966), pp. 768–9.

[13] *Correspondence between Richard Strauss and Hugo von Hofmannsthal* (London, 1961), pp. 32–3.

[14] *The Autobiography of Karl von Dittersdorf*, trans. A. D. Coleridge (London, 1896), pp. 141–5.

[15] *Memoirs of Hector Berlioz*, ed. David Cairns (London, 1969), p. 231.

[16] For a contrary opinion see Jacques Barzun, *Berlioz and the Romantic Century*, 3rd ed. (New York, 1969), vol.i, p. 278, n. 67.

[17] *Louis Spohr's Autobiography* (London, 1865), vol. i, p. 39.

[18] *Reminiscences of Michael Kelly* (London, 1826), vol. i, pp. 258–62.

[19] *The Present State of Music in France and Italy* (London, 1771) and *The Present State of Music in Germany, the Netherlands, and United Provinces*, 2 vols. (London, 1773).

[20] *The Present State of Music in France and Italy*, p. 4.

[21] *The Present State of Music in Germany*, etc., vol. ii, p. 269.

[22] *The Present State of Music in France and Italy*, pp. 325–6.

[23] *Scriptores ecclesiastici de musica*, 3 vols. (St. Blaise, 1784).

[24] *Scriptorum de musica medii aevi nova series*, 4 vols. (Paris, 1864–76).

[25] Modern edition by E. Rohloff (Leipzig, 1943).

[26] Modern edition by Armand Machabey (Paris, 1951).

[27] Facsimile edition by E. H. Fellowes (London, 1937); modern edition by R. A. Harman (London, 1952).

[28] *A Plaine and Easie Introduction to Practicall Musicke*, p. 179 (modern edition, p. 292).

[29] Facsimile edition by R. Eitner (Leipzig, 1896).

[30] Facsimile edition of Part II by W. Gurlitt (Kassel, 1929).

[31] Facsimile edition (Milan, 1934).

[32] Facsimile edition (Milan, 1933); English translation in O. Strunk, *Source Readings in Music History* (New York, 1950).

[33] Facsimile edition by Hans-Peter Schmitz (Kassel, 1953).

[34] English translation by William J. Mitchell (New York, 1949).

[35] For a detailed account see F. T. Arnold, *The Art of Accompaniment from a Thorough-Bass* (London, 1931).

[36] Hans T. David and Arthur Mendel, *The Bach Reader*, 2nd ed. (New York, 1966), p. 329.

[37] *Roger North on Music*, ed. John Wilson (London, 1959).

[38] Hans T. David and Arthur Mendel, *The Bach Reader*, 2nd ed. (New York, 1966), p. 238.

[39] Extracts translated in Strunk, op. cit., pp. 657–72.

[40] Robert Schumann, *Music and Musicians*, translated by Fanny Raymond Ritter, 1st series (London, n.d.), pp. 212–14.

[41] Hector Berlioz *À travers chants* (Paris, 1862), p. 311; translation by Jacques Barzun, *Berlioz and the Romantic Century*, 3rd ed. (New York, 1969), vol. ii, p. 172.

[42] Frank Walker, *Hugo Wolf*, 2nd ed. (London, 1968), pp. 155–6.

[43] *London Music in 1888–89 as heard by Corno di Bassetto* (London, 1937), p. 46.

. [44] Ibid., p. 176 (but cf. p. 186).

[45] Henry Cart de Lafontaine, *The King's Musick* (London, 1909), p. 263.

[46] Otto Erich Deutsch, *Schubert : a Documentary Biography* (London, 1946), pp. 12 foll.

[47] E. F. Rimbault, *The Old Cheque-Book . . . of the Chapel Royal* (London, 1872), pp. 101–4.

[48] Hans T. David and Arthur Mendel, *The Bach Reader*, 2nd ed. (New York, 1966), pp. 88.

CHAPTER III

THE HISTORIANS AND THE PERIODS

So long as musicians were primarily interested in the music of their own time there was no question of writing a history of the art. The English attitude in the late sixteenth century can be seen very clearly in the pages of Thomas Morley (cf. p. 39), who regards most music before his time as old-fashioned or impossibly remote. On the Continent, however, there were signs of an awakening interest in the music of past ages. Speculation about Greek music was one of the strongest factors which went to the creation of the first operas about 1600; and significantly enough it was in 1600 that Sethus Calvisius (Seth Kallwitz), cantor of St. Thomas's, Leipzig, included in his *Exercitationes Musicae* a substantial outline of the history of music, entitled *De origine et progressu musices*. The purpose of this section was to show how music, through the devoted labours of the great men of the past, had "progressed" up to the end of the sixteenth century; but in developing this point of view the author did not hesitate to express his admiration for the earlier masters of the century, such as Josquin des Prés, Clemens non Papa and Lassus. The whole section might be described as a historical essay rather than history, and the same is true of the historical discussion to be found in Praetorius's *Syntagma Musicum* (see p. 40).

It was not until the end of the seventeenth century that a serious attempt was made to write an independent history of music. Wolfgang Caspar Printz's *Historische Beschreibung der edlen Sing- und Klingkunst* appeared in Dresden in 1690. Five years later an Italian, Giovanni Andrea Angelini

Bontempi, published at Perugia his *Historia musica*. This was followed in 1715 by a French work, the *Histoire de la musique, et de ses effets depuis son origine*, compiled by the Abbé Bourdelot and completed by his nephews Pierre and Jacques Bonnet. It is characteristic of the early histories that they devote much attention to speculation about the origins of music, regardless of the fact that this is a subject about which no certain information is possible. Greek mythology and the Bible are both regarded as sources which call for serious discussion. This old-fashioned and basically unscientific attitude is still to be found in Padre Martini's *Storia della musica*, which began to appear in 1757: the first volume deals systematically with successive periods of Biblical history, beginning with "Music from the Creation of Adam to the Flood", continuing with "Music from the Flood to the Birth of Moses", and eventually reaching the time from the reign of King Solomon to the destruction and rebuilding of the temple.

Though these speculations survived till the end of the eighteenth century and even later, there was also a growing realization that history depends on evidence and that no adequate account of the music of the past can be attempted without extensive research. Martin Gerbert's *De cantu et musica sacra* (1774)—a history of church music—is the work of a man who was assiduous in collecting materials, and who ten years later published the first collection of medieval treatises (see p. 38). But the most substantial and elaborate histories of music in the late eighteenth century were the work of Englishmen. Sir John Hawkins's *General History of the Science and Practice of Music*, in four volumes, appeared in 1776.[1] In the same year Charles Burney published the first volume of his *General History of Music*, which was finally completed by the issue of the fourth volume in 1789.[2] Comparison between the two works is inevitable, and was freely made at the time. The result is strongly in Burney's favour. There is no doubt that in his later volumes he utilized Hawkins's researches; but the conception of the work as a whole is original, and much of the illustrative material had been collected by himself during his travels on the Continent. Hawkins, however much he may have enjoyed music, was not a musician. The principal value of his work lies in the industry it displays. An enormous amount of material is presented to the reader: there are substantial translations from theoretical works, many complete musical examples, extracts from original documents, letters and so on. But all this is thrown together without any discrimination or any fear of irrelevance. Chronological treatment is constantly abandoned in the desire to explore some side issue, and even with an index the reader is hard put to it to construct a coherent narrative from what is in fact a well-intentioned jumble. Unfortunately the nineteenth-century reprint made it available to a much wider circle, and it was too often accepted as an authority without any reasonable justification. Burney's work is very different. It is by modern standards ill-balanced, spending far too much time on the ancient world and devoting a disproportionate amount of space to eighteenth-century opera. But the arrangement is clear and logical, the style is distinguished, and throughout the reader is aware that he is following in the steps of someone to whom music was a living art. Modern critics have sometimes taken Burney to task for his prejudices, but the censure is mis-applied: a historian without prejudices would make very dull reading, and Burney's are sufficiently obvious to be innocent. Though he was quite ready to believe that eighteenth-century music was a model of correctness and purity, he was not wholly blind to the merits of older music. He did much to revive interest in the music of Josquin des Prés and drew attention to the work of Robert White 150 years before the publication of *Tudor Church Music*.

The industry shown by eighteenth-century authors in

collecting materials made it increasingly obvious that the writing of musical history was a gigantic undertaking. It is not surprising that more than one writer since that time has failed to complete a projected work. Forkel, the first biographer of Bach, published an *Allgemeine Geschichte der Musik* in two volumes (1788–1801) which did not get beyond the sixteenth century. A similar fate attended the *Geschichte der Musik* by August Wilhelm Ambros, which first began to appear in 1862. When he died in 1876 only three volumes had been published, and the account of the sixteenth century was still incomplete. A fourth volume, prepared from his notes and dealing with Palestrina and his Roman contemporaries, was published posthumously, and this was later supplemented by a fifth volume consisting of musical examples from the fifteenth and sixteenth centuries which Ambros himself had collected. Incomplete as it is, Ambros's history is still a work of unusual distinction, based on the most thorough research into original sources and reflecting the wide culture of its author. Ambros's career answers effectively the popular view that musicologists are not musicians, since he was accomplished both as a pianist and as a composer; and it also exhibits a triumph of tenacity of purpose over obstacles, since for a considerable part of his life he was employed in the Austrian Civil Service and could devote only his leisure to research.

The nineteenth century saw the production of a large number of histories of music, as well as dictionaries and biographies. It was a time when writers were acutely conscious of the significance of great men and tended to see the history of music as a progress from one eminence to another. The theory of evolution, uncritically transferred from its proper sphere to the history of art, encouraged them also to see this progress, or at any rate a substantial part of it, as an upward march from lowly beginnings to splendid heights. The application of the theory of evolution is perhaps seen in its most extravagant form in the three-volume *History of Music to the Time of the Troubadours* by John Frederick Rowbotham (1885–87).[3] His attempt to show that primitive man was originally content with one note (which was G) and subsequently progressed to two and three notes is the purest fantasy; so is the assertion that in instrumental music a "drum stage" was followed by a "pipe stage" and that in turn by a "lyre stage". The main principles of evolutionary theory were also accepted by Sir Hubert Parry in *The Art of Music* (1893, later published as *The Evolution of the Art of Music*) but with a sanity and balanced judgement that remove his arguments from the realm of mere invention and make possible a critical examination of their validity.

The danger of regarding the history of music as a sequence of great men is that we easily fall into the error of using their names to describe a period or a style without any clear idea of the implications. Thus people who are ill-informed about the late eighteenth century often use the adjective "Mozartian" to describe characteristics of style which are in fact common both to Mozart and to his contemporaries. It is no doubt convenient to speak of the "Bach-Handel period", but the term may easily create confusion of thought unless we know from the first exactly what it implies. If we use it with any pretension to accuracy we mean two things: first, a period of which Bach and Handel are now seen to have been the most eminent men; and second, a period in which certain processes of thought, certain forms and so on were common to a large number of composers, including Bach and Handel. The pursuit of this definition will lead us to consider how far Bach and Handel were different from other composers, and how far they were different from each other.

A period has therefore a significance quite apart from the great men who lived in it. We may define a period in general as a time when composers tend to be inspired by ideals materially different from those of an earlier time, or when old processes of thought have had their day. These changes in style have sometimes been deplored by sentimental historians. They speak, for example, of the "decline of the madrigal"—as though composers might have been expected to continue writing madrigals from the early seventeenth century down to the present day. Such changes are inevitable and healthy: if they did not occur composition would become (as it sometimes has become) merely an imitation of the letter without the spirit—a form of art to which the Germans have given the expressive name *Kapellmeistermusik*. With this proviso our definition of a period is simple and obvious enough. On the other hand there is no absolute unanimity about specific periods, nor can we exactly determine where they begin or where they end: if we could we should make nonsense of the principle of continuity. In general we may say that a term which indicates a style is preferable to one that merely describes a particular technique. Thus, provided we know what we mean by "baroque" it is preferable to speak of the "baroque period" than to follow Hugo Riemann and speak of the "figured bass period". The difficulties, in any case, are considerable; but some form of periodization is essential, if only for the purpose of dividing the material into manageable sections and clarifying our own minds.

Unfortunately this simple, practical necessity has often been confused with a desire to interpret the facts in accordance with particular doctrines. The application of evolutionary theory has induced authors to regard a period as a time of steady progress from small, or even insignificant, beginnings to heights of supreme mastery. The method is seen in its most grotesque form in the *History of Music* by Sir Charles Stanford and Cecil Forsyth. The chapter on the fifteenth and early sixteenth centuries (the work of Forsyth, who wrote the greater part of the book) contains an extraordinary passage on the pupils of Josquin des Prés:

> The characteristic of this whole group is an aversion from the frightful mechanical ingenuities of Josquin and his fellow-workers. This aversion becomes more noticeable in the group of men that immediately succeeded them. And we may be thankful that it was so. For these men cleared away the choking masses of blind-weed that lay on the foot-hills leading upwards to the heights of Palestrina.[4]

This is extraordinary for three reasons. First of all, it is historically inaccurate. The work of Josquin is not marked by "frightful mechanical ingenuities", and no one who had given even a casual glance at his music could imagine that it was. Secondly, it is a pure assumption that Palestrina was immeasurably superior to all his predecessors. Thirdly, the metaphor is nonsensical and appears to be designed merely to give verisimilitude to an untenable proposition. In fact Forsyth becomes intoxicated by metaphor to the extent of abandoning both reason and probability. The chapter ends by warning us not to imagine

> that the muddy stream of misplaced ingenuity dried up suddenly with Josquin's death. On the contrary, it continued to flow for many years. But it was not the main stream. And its impurities were only a fleck on the surface when it met the big tidal-wave that brought Palestrina's galleon up to her anchorage.[5]

The mechanical ingenuity has now become a muddy stream, and Palestrina has exchanged a mountain top for a ship. By the next chapter he has acquired a new means of locomotion:

> It is true that the two pairs of brothers Nanini and Anerio rode in Palestrina's chariot. But, when Palestrina dropped the reins, it was at the top of a hill. The new drivers thought, no

doubt, that there was a long stretch of level road in front of them. But certain cunning eyes in Italy saw even then that the grade was imperceptibly downhill and was likely to end in a quagmire.[6]

Absurdity could go no further.

Equally misguided is the attempt to establish an artificial sequence of the arts. Cecil Gray, in his book *Predicaments, or Music and the Future* (London, 1936), sees the centuries dominated respectively by architecture, sculpture, painting, literature and music. The argument is advanced that "during the period of the ascendancy of one particular art, the other arts aspire towards the aesthetic ideals embodied in that leading art".[7] The language is clumsy but the meaning is clear. It follows that Dante's *Divina Commedia* is architectural, "like a vast Gothic cathedral", Chaucer's *Canterbury Tales* are pictorial, the operas of Monteverdi and Gluck are literary, while even Mozart, "pure musician though he was in a sense, lives for us today primarily by virtue of his operas".[8] We might be tempted to ask in what sense Mozart was a pure musician, or to question whether we should ignore him if he had not written operas. We might suggest that operatic libretti are not the same thing as literature. We might even go so far as to suggest that when the author tells us that "the central date" of the Gothic style "is round about 1100" he is talking nonsense. But these are minor criticisms. The principal objection is simply that the facts of history have been manipulated to fit a preconceived pattern. It is no justification of the pattern to say that it is neatly arranged: it is the very neatness which inspires suspicion. And when we find that every century bristles with individual examples which reduce the theory to mere wool-gathering, it is time to call a halt.

A near relative of the theory of the sequence of the arts is the doctrine of cycles. According to Alfred Lorenz[9] a pendulum swings at regular intervals from homophony, rational rhythm, subjectivity and emotion on the one hand to polyphony, irrational rhythm, objectivity and reason on the other. In its motion it naturally passes through periods of transition. The decisive points of change occur at intervals of 300 years, beginning about A.D. 400. According to Lorenz's diagram we should now be in the middle of a transition period from homophony to polyphony. If the theory were sound, it would be convenient, since one could then safely predict the future of music until at least A.D. 2200, if not further. But like most symmetrical patterns it can only be constructed at the cost of ignoring everything that goes to prove it false. It makes nonsense, for instance, to say that 1510 was one of the furthest points of the swing to polyphony, since this was a time when homophonic part-songs enjoyed a great vogue: just as 300 years later plenty of polyphonic music was being written by Beethoven and his contemporaries. The theory, like most theories of this kind, is a product of wishful thinking. It is quite possible to survey past history in this way, but it can be done only by imitating Nelson and putting the telescope to one's blind eye.

Though the division of musical history into periods is convenient for the purposes of a continuous narrative, it is not the only method. Hermann Kretzschmar, for instance, edited a series of ten volumes entitled *Kleine Handbücher der Musikgeschichte nach Gattungen* (Leipzig, 1905–22) in which the division is by forms: one volume deals with the oratorio, another with the concerto, another with the motet, and so on. The advantages of this method are obvious. The continuity of musical forms may be obscure unless we can study all the stages in their development. Bach's motets may seem, to a superficial eye, to have nothing to do with the motet in the thirteenth century: Elgar's oratorios may appear to have only a slender connexion with Handel's. By examining the intermediate stages we discover the imperceptible process by which forms change—a process depending not merely on the individuality of composers but on the environment in which they grow up. The disadvantages of the method are equally obvious. The separation of opera from the symphony, for instance, is purely artificial: each nourished the other. The study of a form in isolation may easily foster the illusion that its growth was a spontaneous development, remote from the circumstances in which other departments of the art were rooted and flourished.

The ten volumes of the *Handbuch der Musikwissenschaft* edited by Ernst Bücken (Potsdam, 1928–31) make the best of both worlds. Six volumes are devoted to periods—ancient and oriental music, the Middle Ages and the Renaissance, baroque music, and so on—while a further two deal with Catholic and Protestant church music respectively. In addition there is a volume devoted to aesthetics and form and another on methods of performance (*Aufführungspraxis*), and the first volume also includes a substantial section on instruments. The only objection to this scheme is that there is a considerable amount of overlapping. This would not matter if additional volumes had been devoted to other specific branches of music (which may well have been the editor's original intention). But as it stands the work pays a disproportionate amount of attention to church music.

Another, less serious, objection is that the excellent volume on the Middle Ages and the Renaissance (the work of Heinrich Besseler) compresses more into the space than is desirable in a work of this scope. If the baroque period is to have a volume to itself, it is equally important that the Middle Ages should receive a similar treatment. The problems raised by the titles of the volumes are another matter, which is necessarily more controversial. When, for instance, did the Renaissance begin? What, if any, are its boundaries? There is no absolute unanimity on this point, and in the last resort we are driven to read the volume to see what interpretation the editor, or the author, has adopted. There is less difference of opinion about the terms "baroque" and "rococo", both of which figure in the titles of Bücken's publication. The terms are borrowed from architecture and were first used in a disparaging sense, just as "Gothic" was once assumed to mean "barbarous". The application of these terms to music is recent and is based on the assumption that at any period there are certain basic similarities between the arts, not because practitioners of different arts necessarily copy each other but because all arts are a product of the same environment and exist in the same society. The pompous splendour of baroque architecture has its counterpart in much of the music of Lully, Purcell, Handel and Bach, just as the delicacy of rococo painting can be related to the late eighteenth-century minuet or *divertimento*. The parallel must not be pushed too far. The expressive recitative of seventeenth-century opera, for example, can be matched in literature, but hardly in architecture. But so long as the terms are used in the broadest and most general sense, they do no harm; and for most musicians today they certainly have a far more definite sense than such vague expressions as "pre-classical" or "classical".

The subdivisions of the *Oxford History of Music* also call for some comment. This work, which began to appear in 1901, was the first history of music to be produced by a team of contributors. The first two volumes, by H. Ellis Wooldridge, cover roughly the same ground as Besseler's volume on the Middle Ages and the Renaissance, though the treatment is entirely different and, naturally enough, the later work was able to profit by the intensive research devoted to medieval music during the intervening years. Wooldridge's volumes bear the title "The Polyphonic Period". It is at first sight not an unreasonable title, since the development of polyphony as a means of artistic expression figures prominently in the history of the period. But as a description of the period it is obviously inadequate, since other periods also cultivated polyphony; in fact the conception of musical texture as a combination of independent lines has never been abandoned and is still accepted today. The centuries before 1600 could only be described as *the* polyphonic period if a limited and arbitrary interpretation were given to the word "polyphony". Furthermore, a great deal of the music before 1600 is not "polyphonic" in this sense. Quite apart from the songs of the troubadours, Minnesinger and Meistersinger, and the lute-songs of the sixteenth century, there is plenty of secular music which is homophonic in treatment; and even in the field of church music—for example, in the Old Hall manuscript of the fifteenth century—we find pieces which are little more than harmonizations of plainsong melodies. The idea that sixteenth-century music was wholly polyphonic in conception can be refuted by looking at the bass parts of almost any collection of madrigals: over and over again one finds a bass with no more significant function than to act as a harmonic support to the other voices.

The fourth volume of the *Oxford History of Music*, published in 1902, is called "The Age of Bach and Handel". We have already discussed (p. 53) the implications of this title. Even if we are aware of those implications it is still open to criticism. The period corresponding to the lives of Bach and Handel is not necessarily a decisive one, and also there is a good deal of music composed within that period which differs radically from the traditions accepted by Bach and Handel respectively. The most notable example is Bach's second son, Carl Philipp Emanuel, who was thirty-six years old when his father died and already by that time a fully-fledged composer. Within his lifetime, as Hadow points out,[10] fall both Bach's cantata *Ich hatte viel Bekümmernis* (1714) and Mozart's "Jupiter" symphony (1788). There is more justification for speaking of "The Age of Beethoven" —the title of the eighth volume of the *New Oxford History of Music* (now in course of publication)—since Beethoven was not only the dominating figure of his time but was accepted as such by nineteenth-century composers. It is not extravagant to say that he towered so high that he threw a shadow over the work of many of his successors. Yet even here we may lose a sense of proportion. Schubert's career coincides with the latter part of Beethoven's; but there is nothing in his work to suggest that he was ever dominated by the older man's example, much as he admired him. And there is plenty of music of this period by French and Italian composers which owes nothing to Beethoven. If anything, the influence is the other way round: there is no mistaking the impression made on Beethoven by the music of Cherubini.

More important than the titles of volumes are the divisions between them. Both the *Oxford History of Music* and Bücken's series divide roughly at 1600. This is in many ways a convenient date. It coincides with the appearance of opera—a new form which rapidly conquered Europe and had a decisive influence on the development of music in general. It marks the time when composers began systematically to use a harmonized bass to supply the lower parts of a vocal or instrumental ensemble or to support a solo voice or instrument. It marks also the growth of a passion for virtuosity which invaded all fields of musical performance. At the same time it is easy to exaggerate the nature of the change and to attach too much importance to a single date. In England, for example, the year 1600 has no special significance. Most of the English madrigals and lute-songs were published after that date, and the new style did not appear in church music until the Restoration. For this reason the division adopted in the *New Oxford History* is more satisfactory: the fourth volume of that work covers roughly the period from 1540 to 1630. The first date corresponds with the beginning of the Italian madrigal; the second with the opening of public opera houses in Venice and the outbreak of the Civil War in England, both of which, for different reasons, were decisive events. The title of the volume is "The Age of Humanism"—a title which places music in its proper relation to the art, literature and scholarship of the time.

Wherever we draw lines across the history of music, we are faced with problems. The first appearance of harmonized music is obviously of great importance, but it is very difficult to say precisely when it occurred. We know that the first written records date from the ninth century. But the fact that simple harmony, the use of a drone bass and even canon are found in the music of primitive peoples today suggests very strongly that these practices are not necessarily the product of Western civilization—that there may, in fact, be an ancient tradition of popular music-making behind the first appearance of systematic polyphony in the music of the Western church. Again, it would be convenient if we could fix a time at which the modern conception of harmony as a sequence of related chords could be said to have invaded the tradition of independent part-writing. It is conventional to say that this happened in the course of the sixteenth century; but English music of about 1300 shows plenty of examples in which there is the simplest possible harmonic sequence. It is impossible to suppose that musicians wrote a series of what we now call first inversions without being aware of the chords as such or of their relation to each other. More complex but equally convincing examples are to be found in the music of the fifteenth century. Again, one of the decisive changes in musical style is the supersession of baroque polyphony in the eighteenth century by the *style galant*, where the emphasis was on pointed rhythms and clearly defined melodies heard above a simple and symmetrical accompaniment. But it is not too easy to say when this change occurred. Certainly it had begun long before

the death of Bach, who was regarded by some at least of his
contemporaries as a turgid and old-fashioned composer
(cf. p. 42).

In every change of style old fashions persist for a long
time beside the new. This is very evident in twentieth-century
music. There is little in common between Strauss's *Der
Rosenkavalier*, Sibelius's fourth symphony, Stravinsky's
Petrouchka and Ravel's *L'Heure espagnole*; yet all these works
appeared in the year 1911, not to mention Elgar's second
symphony, Scriabin's *Prometheus*, Mahler's *Das Lied von
der Erde* (posthumously) and Wolf-Ferrari's *Jewels of the
Madonna*. And a year later Schönberg's *Five Orchestral
Pieces* had their first performance. Opera in the early seventeenth century was far less an innovation than is commonly
supposed. The style of declamatory song—its melodic pathos,
its abrupt changes of harmony—owed much to the madrigal.
In Monteverdi's *Orfeo* (1607), the most distinguished
example of the form, not only the madrigal but also the
motet and the instrumental ensemble music of the sixteenth
century have clearly been a powerful influence. A revolution
in music is in fact impossible, since previous experience
cannot at one stroke be obliterated from our consciousness.

The difficulty of defining exactly the characteristics of any
period is seen most clearly if we try to establish the outstanding features of our own time. It is true that a later age will
probably see distinct resemblances where we see wholly
independent styles, and it is also true that twentieth-
century composers are much less inclined than their predecessors in the eighteenth century to accept a common
idiom. But even if we make allowance for these considerations, we shall still be acutely aware of the difficulty of
establishing a coherent pattern. The exact relationship of
the twentieth century to the nineteenth is often a matter
for dispute. Is impressionism, for example, an independent
growth or is it merely a development of romanticism?

Future historians may be able to be more dogmatic about
these matters when they see the picture of the complete
century. But it is equally possible that the passage of time
will blur for them some of the sharp outlines of which we are
conscious today.

The differences between the music of one age and the
next are not simple. There are differences in technique, in
approach, in environment. Music is affected by the circles
for which it is intended: it may be written for a cultured
aristocracy, for the great public of music-lovers, or for a
mutual admiration society. Though its appeal is the same for
every age, there is always a difference in the terms in which
emotion is expressed. In consequence, though it may
continue to give delight to music-lovers of succeeding ages,
it can never mean exactly the same to them as it did to
those who first heard it. Our environment, our reactions, our
first impressions are different from those of our forefathers.
The music which comes to us from the past has to pass
through the veil of our own experience; and that experience
includes our consciousness of many other kinds of music.
We have to deal with an elusive, intangible art. We might be
tempted to cry, with Shelley, "Rarely, rarely comest thou,
spirit of delight". The miracle is that it comes so often.

[1] A second edition, in two volumes, was published in 1875.
[2] A second edition, in two volumes, edited by Frank Mercer, was
published in 1935.
[3] An extract is quoted in Warren Dwight Allen, *Philosophies of
Music History* (New York, 1939), pp. 111–12.
[4] Charles Villiers Stanford and Cecil Forsyth, *A History of Music*
(London, 1916), p. 155.
[5] Ibid., p. 157.
[6] Ibid., p. 173.
[7] *Predicaments*, p. 58.
[8] Ibid., pp. 58–61.
[9] *Abendländische Musikgeschichte im Rhythmus der Generationen*
(Berlin, 1928).
[10] *The Viennese Period* (Oxford, 1904), p. 68.

CHAPTER IV

THE SOCIAL BACKGROUND

WE have now to consider in more detail the relation between music and the social conditions in which it thrives. This is a subject which is often suspected by historians in general as frivolous and by musicians as unnecessary. History is too often regarded merely as the record of political and social changes, and the arts as merely incidental: if they are discussed at all, it is rare to find in such a discussion any intelligent understanding of the part played by music. References to music in general histories are frequently perfunctory and based on out-of-date authorities. Musicians, on the other hand, are apt to regard music as a phenomenon separable from life. Both these attitudes are open to criticism. In the first place, music is one of the ways in which man's nature expresses itself, and it is sometimes so closely bound up with human existence that a discussion of it cannot possibly be regarded as irrelevant to the history of mankind. Its association with religious cults is ancient and continuous: its efficacy in therapeutic treatment, once thought of as merely superstition, is now taken for granted. In certain circumstances it has the power to inflame political passions and to strengthen the unity of a common purpose. "Lilliburlero" and the "Marseillaise" are examples of songs so infectious that they did not merely express solidarity: they helped to create it. Even opera has been known to have this effect. When Auber's *La Muette de Portici* was performed in Brussels in 1830 it helped to launch the revolution which created the independence of Belgium. Musicians themselves have often expressed political aspirations: Beethoven's sympathy with

C

the advanced liberalism of his day is well known. They have also served ideologies—at the time of the French Revolution, for example, or in Russia today. Some of them have even taken part in political activity, though Wagner's brief and inglorious career as a revolutionary can hardly be regarded as an encouragement to others. Often the relation between music and society is less precise but no less obvious. The extraordinary popularity of serious music in England during the 1939–45 war was not an accident. It demonstrated the power of music to provide an antidote to the austerity and the hazards of the time.

In the second place, music is not something which appears out of the blue. It is coloured by the individual's experience and upbringing: it is also evidence of character, which is itself partly a product of environment. It is true that the acceptance of this view has sometimes led to extravagance. Elgar's second symphony, for example, is often referred to as a "picture of the Edwardian age". It is difficult to see how any single work could be so comprehensive, and in fact we know that this symphony is nothing of the kind.[1] It is rather a self-portrait. But at the same time the terms in which it is expressed are characteristic of a particular period and would be inconceivable at any other.

Style is not wholly a product of musical development: it results also from the impact of ideas. We can illustrate this by comparing three operas—Mozart's *Figaro* (1786), Beethoven's *Fidelio* (1805) and Strauss's *Salome* (1905). *Figaro* deals with a revolutionary subject (though the opera is considerably milder than Beaumarchais's play). The modern listener, entranced by the wit and charm of Mozart's music, may not realize how subversive is the story. But once we dismiss from our minds any illusions created by the eighteenth-century flavour of the music, we can see how strong, even brutal, is Mozart's delineation of character. This is, in fact, a contemporary work: the characters are men and

women of his day. Yet for all its rebellion against the social
order it belongs to a period before the storm burst on Europe.
How Mozart might have reacted to the French Revolution
it is not possible to say. *Fidelio* shows us how Beethoven
reacted: it is a work which is both highly personal and
characteristic of its time, owing allegiance to a treatment
already established in France. It is as up to date and pertinent
for its period as Menotti's *The Consul* in the twentieth
century. The events which it portrays are not fantasy but a
record of actual experience. It is not, like *Figaro*, a mere
protest against feudalism: it is a passionate assertion of the
belief that tyranny and the cruelty of force are powerless
against the heroism of a woman's love. The music, no
less than the text, proclaims this belief and has no need to
strive for sympathy, since everything it portrays is known
to be true. *Salome* is equally a product of its time. Oscar
Wilde's play, patently inferior to Flaubert's short story on
the same subject, is an example of *fin-de-siècle* decadence so
characteristic that the modern reader can hardly peruse it
without a smile. Strauss matches the text with music which
drips with the same voluptuous rottenness, but oddly mixes
with it a homely and characteristically German idiom. Such
a setting would have been impossible at any other time or in
any other country.

All these works are operas. Yet the term "opera" has
very different associations at different periods. In the early
seventeenth century it had no meaning at all other than
"work". Only gradually was the expression *opera in musica*
applied to music drama, until eventually the single word
"opera" was thought to be self-sufficient. The differences in
conception are often striking. What is there in common
between the operas of Handel and Wagner, of Gluck and
Puccini? The differences are not only those of technique and
idiom, nor do they result simply from a different approach
to the problems of writing opera. They arise also from the

type of audience that composers are writing for or wish
to create, and from different conceptions of the way in which
character should be presented on the stage. The same is true
of church music. The term embraces music as diverse as
twelfth-century *organa*, Palestrina's Masses, the *St. Matthew
Passion*, Mozart's Requiem and Stainer's *Crucifixion*. What
is the common denominator between these works?

The historian demands, not merely what sort of men wrote
this music but what sort of people they were writing for.
He is driven to face the dilemma that the art of one age is
sometimes not merely incomprehensible but even intolerable
to another. Easy generalization ignores these barriers. The
songs of the troubadours or the English lutenists, Schubert's
Lieder and Poulenc's *mélodies* are all treated as songs, regardless of the wholly different environment in which they came
to birth: dance music becomes a category which is forced to
comprise the medieval *estampie*, the *ballet de cour* in France,
the *deutscher Tanz* of Mozart's Salzburg, the reign of the
waltz and the lancers, and the vogue of the rumba.

There is no single, universal cause which brings music
to birth: the factors are many and varied. They may include
the demands of an accepted religion, the vanity of a patron,
the pride of a community or the rebellion of an individual.
There are even cases where composers successfully challenge
their environment and create a new world. Handel did it
with the English oratorio, Wagner with opera. But even here
environment plays its part. Every composer is sensitive to
his musical environment, and this in turn is dependent on a
host of local or national conditions, perhaps also on national
temperament, which is itself affected by climate. A composer,
like everyone else, is influenced by the music he hears as a
boy: this is as true of Purcell as of Bach, of Mozart as of
Wagner. But the extent of the influence will depend on the
conditions which make possible the hearing of music and on
the types of music available. The appearance of a genius may

be thwarted by circumstances: in certain societies the opportunities for a general musical education are limited. The
nature of the influence will also depend on the immediate
contacts which are made in early years. At one period a boy
may approach music through the accident of having a good
voice; at another he may turn into an opera composer because
he was able to get into the gallery of a theatre for a few pence.
A composer may rebel against convention, but he cannot
annihilate his early experiences; he may learn much in later
life, but something is always "given", in the sense that he
builds on a foundation which he did not choose and which
he was incapable of avoiding. A work like *Tristan*, though
new in its forms of expression, arises in a society where opera
is already a convention. Through repetition its idiom becomes
familiar. Young German composers are reared on it, and for
them it can never have the slightly exotic flavour that it still
has in England, where it has never been a standard item in
the operatic repertory.

The history of art-forms is rooted in social conditions.
The cultivation of oratorio in England is due to the continued popularity of Handel in the nineteenth century—a
popularity which he helped to establish himself by his
performances of *Messiah* in aid of the Foundling Hospital.
An additional reason was the view held by the Victorians that
oratorio was edifying, though here too one could cite Handel
as a precedent. Congratulated by a noble lord on the entertainment afforded by one of his oratorios, he replied that he
wished not merely to entertain but to make people better.
Yet at the same time his oratorios had the strictly practical
purpose of meeting the local conditions of eighteenth-century
London. Realizing that opera had ceased to be a paying
proposition he turned to oratorio as an alternative and more
lucrative source. Though in Handel's hands it acquired a
new and individual character, oratorio as a form was already
established. It was originally a product of the Counter-

Reformation, beginning with an association of edifying drama and vernacular hymns: and the vernacular hymns in turn go back to the thirteenth century, when Italy sought expiation for worldly disasters in flagellation, and pilgrims sang as they made violent repentance. We have here a chain of causes which leads eventually to *The Dream of Gerontius* and *Belshazzar's Feast*.

In some cases particular types of music are the direct result of circumstances. Anglican church music, for instance, has its immediate origin in Henry VIII's breach with the Papacy. To this political manœuvre we owe the English cathedral service—a form of music which has no exact parallel anywhere. English ballad opera is another example. It began in the early eighteenth century as a satire against society and a challenge to the fashionable supremacy of Italian opera in London, and rapidly became an established English form, exchanging in time the convention of borrowed melodies for entirely original music. Sullivan's comic operas, which are largely unintelligible abroad, were its eventual heirs and one of the most characteristic features of late nineteenth-century music in England: it is significant that a German historian[2] has singled them out as England's most important contribution to the music of the period. But for all its Englishness the ballad opera had also a continental progeny. Imitated in Germany it became the begetter of the *Singspiel*, which in turn developed a history of its own in different social conditions. It is perhaps too bald a simplification to say that *The Beggar's Opera* was responsible for Mozart's *Die Entführung*, but the chain which links the two is plainly discernible.

Conventions of style and medium may also owe their origin to particular circumstances. The reason why the classical symphony so often begins loud is that it grew out of the opera overture, and the opera overture had to assert itself in the face of a clamorous audience which was interested mainly in singers. The overture to *Figaro* is original in that it refuses to accept this convention; and naturally when opera became much more a cult and much less a popular entertainment a quiet beginning was even more feasible: *Lohengrin* and *Aida* are examples. But by that time the symphony and opera had gone different ways, and the original connexion had been entirely forgotten. The orchestra, again, might seem at first sight to be a curious assemblage of different instruments, providing an ensemble which experience has proved effective but in no way self-evidently the best or only possible combination. The explanation here is to be found in the history of patronage. Magnificent establishments maintained players on every available orchestral instrument, and once opera suggested the need for a standard organization it was natural to use the strings, which were most suitable for the purpose, as the foundation. The science of orchestration, subsequently developed, was a rationalization of the resources: the materials had long been available. It is equally interesting to see how the organ, which was originally a purely secular instrument, came to be used in cathedrals simply because it was the most suitable instrument for sustaining voices in a large and resonant building. Once established as the normal instrument for worship, it acquired sacred associations, so that when it was introduced into the cinema in the twentieth century there were many who regarded its employment for a secular purpose as desecration. The by-products of its use in church are too numerous to mention.

Whether music flourishes as an art depends on the existence of favourable social conditions and on economic considerations. It is not necessarily a matter of taste, though that may very well come to take command in a prosperous community (see pp. 135 foll.). Unsettled conditions may leave their mark on composition, but they do not favour widespread performance; or alternatively they may exclude some categories in favour of others. The flowering of music in well-to-do circles in Elizabethan England was possible in a society which was no longer rent by faction. In this world a new domestic architecture grew up, and the new order of squirearchy: and here too we find the new type of amateur, anxious not to compete with professionals but devoted to the private practice of the art. Sometimes the results of political disturbance are unexpected. The Puritan revolution, by suppressing cathedral choirs, encouraged the cultivation of secular music. The Puritans also taught people to read music for the purpose of singing hymns, and so laid the foundations of a wider musical education which bore fruit in the later seventeenth century. Where there are long traditions temporary set-backs have no lasting effect: English church music at the Restoration recovered rapidly from its suppression during the Commonwealth. Where there are no traditions the plant takes time to grow: we can see this in the United States, where a multitude of influxes from the Old World are only now beginning to produce a characteristically American music. The student of musical history may not always be fully aware of these differences in tradition and environment; but they have a far-reaching effect on the development of music in different countries. It is not merely that the associations of common terms such as "opera", "song" and "oratorio" are different. There are also radical differences in taste. It is not enough to observe that the French dislike Brahms and the English are suspicious of Mahler. The causes of these reactions are deep-seated and go far to explain the diversity to be found in European musical culture. At the same time it is true that national differences were not always as strongly marked as they are today. Music was far more international in the eighteenth century. No organization was necessary to make it so: it was merely that the same canons of good taste were common to the wealthy classes of all countries, whatever local differences of style there might be. Today Europe is one in point of communications but not in culture, whereas in the fifteenth century Dunstable, an English composer, won his reputation on the Continent.

To some extent popular music plays its part in shaping traditions; but until the nineteenth century its effect on the general development of music was limited. The reason for this was that cultured people in general despised it. It was accepted only in a patronizing way, and in the hands of musicians was so stylized that it became a wholly sophisticated form of art. The dance movements in the seventeenth-century suite can be traced back to their humble originals, but in their court dress they are far removed from the world of their ancestors. A new awareness of popular music began to appear in the nineteenth century. The collection of folk songs and folk dances brought with it the realization that popular tradition had something to offer to musicians. To a Romantic artist, eager to escape from his immediate environment, folk song, like plainsong, could have an irresistible attraction. The nineteenth century saw also a levelling of taste among all sections of the community, so that popular music was no longer something to be despised or merely patronized by a minority but something which could be frankly enjoyed for its own sake.

[1] For the detailed evidence see W. H. Temple Gairdner, *W.H.T.G. to his Friends* (London, 1930), p. 157.
[2] Alfred Einstein, *Music in the Romantic Era* (New York, 1947), pp. 291-2.

CHAPTER V

THE INFLUENCE OF THE CHURCH

ONE of the most potent influences on the development of music has been its association with the Church. This association is natural. From the earliest times, so far as we know, music has been regarded as a natural part of religious worship. It has, in fact, a close association with magic—an association which has left its mark on the English language. Our word "enchant" comes from the Latin *incantare*, "to sing a magical song over someone"; "charm" is derived from *carmen*, "a song". The magical element persists in all religious worship, since religion is not simply a rule of life but communication with the supernatural. Hence music figures largely in the worship of the Jewish synagogue and was naturally imitated by the early Christian church. One of the earliest references in pagan literature to Christian worship occurs in a letter from the younger Pliny, then governor of Bithynia, to the Emperor Trajan about A.D. 113. His description seems to imply the practice of antiphonal singing—a practice which has survived in psalm-singing down to the present day. But antiphonal singing was not an invention of the Christians. Its practice by the Therapeutae, a Jewish sect, is described by Philo of Alexandria, who was born about A.D. 20. According to his account

All at once on both sides rise up . . . and form two choirs, the one of men, the other of women. Each choir chooses as its leader and cantor one who is distinguished as well by the dignity of his person as by his skill in music. Then they sing hymns to God, composed in different metres and melodies, sometimes all together, sometimes answering one another in a skilful manner.[1]

This association of men and women in song seems to have been maintained also in the Christian church in the early centuries of our era. Before long, however, women were prohibited from taking part in the chant and were replaced by boys: this change occurred at least as early as the fourth century. Since singing in the church was now a male prerogative the monasteries became "the headquarters of psalmody".[2]

The adoption of music as a part of Christian worship had three important results: first, the creation of a type of music suitable for the purpose; second, the training of singers and the employment of expert musicians in choirs; third, a constant suspicion that music, as a sensuous art, might abuse its function as an aid to religion. Something of the magical character of primitive worship survives in plainsong, or Gregorian chant, though the repertory also includes a number of hymns of simple character, suitable for everyone to sing. Plainsong is by its very nature opposed to secular music: it eschews neatly symmetrical rhythms, it allows for ecstasy, it suggests mystery. Its early history shows the existence of many local varieties, since the rapid spread of the Church through Europe encouraged diversity. Uniformity was established only as the central authority of Rome was imposed on all branches of the Church. A typical injunction occurs in the orders made by the Council of Clovesho in England in 747:

[The festivals of our Lord] . . . in the Office of Baptism, the celebration of Masses, in the method of chanting, shall be celebrated in one and the same way, namely, in accordance with the sample that we have received in writing from the Roman Church.[3]

The reference to a sample received in writing suggests that some form of musical notation was already in use. Notation was clearly a necessity if uniformity was to be established, since it would have been difficult to maintain a purely oral tradition in centres far removed from Rome. It was thus in some measure a guarantee against the corruption of the chant and an obstacle to local variations. We can therefore say with certainty that we owe our musical notation in the first place to the Church: its adoption for secular purposes was a natural consequence.

The association of boys and men involved singing in octaves. It is possible that some singers found it convenient to sing the melodies at an intermediate pitch, which would thus result in parallel movement in fourths and fifths. This is the type of polyphony described in *Musica enchiriadis* in the ninth century (see p. 38). As we have seen already (p. 62), there is no means of knowing when the practice began or to what extent it had its roots in popular traditions of music-making. It is also quite possible that singing in fourths and fifths was suggested by the fact that on the medieval organ these intervals could be played simultaneously simply by drawing the appropriate registers. The fact that such part-singing was called *organum*, which is clearly not a technical term but a popular name, is suggestive; on the other hand *organum* can mean any instrument, not necessarily the organ. There are other theories about the origins of polyphony in western Europe, but none of them can be regarded as certain. What is certain is that the systematic adoption and development of polyphony was the work of church musicians, who saw in it a natural means of elaborating the chant, just as the medieval builders came to devise a more elaborate style of church architecture. Before long the same methods were employed in secular composition, which in turn came to influence the style of church music. It is, in fact, quite possible that Gregorian chant, in spite of its deliberate avoidance of secular rhythms, was from the first affected by the melodic idioms of secular song. Later, when the corpus of church melodies had become established, the influence seems to have worked the other way. The presence of Gregorian idioms in twelfth-century troubadour music suggests that the minds of cultured people were thoroughly soaked in the melodies which they heard in church, just as they were also sensitive to the charm and vitality of popular song.

The music of every period shows how false and unreal is a rigid and arbitrary distinction between sacred and secular music. Music is not in itself either sacred or secular: it becomes so by force of associations, which may very well create the illusion that particular styles are appropriate to the church and the chamber respectively. In later music secular influences on church music are often strongly marked. The late sixteenth-century motet was clearly affected by the madrigal: it often shows the same subjective approach, the same desire to translate the essence of the words into music, the same expressive use of dissonance and even of chromaticism. In the eighteenth century there are also close correspondences. We know that in some cases Bach bodily transferred instrumental movements to his church cantatas and turned them into choruses; and quite apart from these specific instances there are many movements in the cantatas which strongly suggest the influence of the orchestral concerto. The same is true of recitative. There is no valid distinction to be drawn between the style of the recitative in Bach's secular cantatas and that in the church cantatas and the Passions. Both derive from the current practice of opera composers. The same close association is often to be found in the arias as well.

Since medieval education was the concern of the Church, it was natural that provision should be made for training musicians to take their part in church services. The monasteries, as we have seen, were the centres where singers received the necessary instruction, and where composition was actively practised. And since the singers were called upon to fulfil liturgical functions it was common for them to be priests. Many distinguished composers were in fact in orders: Machaut is an example from the fourteenth century, Dufay from the fifteenth. Palestrina himself intended to enter the priesthood after the death of his first wife, but married again before he had taken the decisive step. It would, however, have been difficult to maintain cathedral services adequately if only priests had been employed. Hence the practice of using lay singers as well, many of whom won equal eminence as composers. Since there was much competition for their services the status of church singers was high: the Papal chapel, in particular, was served by some of the most eminent musicians in Europe. It is significant that *castrati* (or *evirati*) were used by the Roman Church before they were ever introduced into opera, indeed before opera had been invented—there was certainly one in the Pope's chapel in 1562. This may possibly indicate that there was difficulty in getting a sufficient supply of experienced boys; or it may have been due to a desire to make permanent what would otherwise have been merely temporary services. Quite apart from the introduction of *castrati* we cannot help noticing how the exclusion of women from church choirs resulted in a particular style of writing for the soprano voice in church music which has persisted down to the present day.

The Church, whether Catholic or Protestant, has been one of the most powerful patrons in the history of music, not from any particular desire to encourage music as an art but simply because music was accepted as a necessary enrichment of the liturgy. The only exception is to be found in certain Reformed sects which virtually excluded music altogether. It follows that any reduction or withdrawal of the Church's patronage was bound to have an unfortunate economic effect. This is precisely what happened in England in the sixteenth and seventeenth centuries, first through the suppression of the monasteries and even more later through the Puritan revolution. In the latter case large numbers of excellent musicians employed in the Chapel Royal and the cathedrals were thrown out of employment and were forced to exist on teaching or the generosity of private patrons.

The Church gave employment to composers as well as singers. They too had their duties to perform; and the practical result was a mass of music of which only a fraction is known today. The particular traditions of the Catholic and Protestant churches had diverse results, but the principle remains the same. We owe the existence of Bach's church cantatas and Passions to the conditions of Lutheran worship at St. Thomas's, Leipzig: they were written not to satisfy a need for self-expression but simply to answer a demand. The influence of a church may also extend beyond its walls. In England the cathedral has often played an important part in musical life, with the organist acting as an animator of local music, and the cathedral choir as an educative force. The Three Choirs Festival, founded in 1729, is an illustration of this principle on a larger scale. Originally the cathedral choirs of Worcester, Gloucester and Hereford met alternately in one of the three cities; but the festivals soon developed into a union of choral singers from each of the centres, and so made possible the composition and performance of substantial choral works with orchestral accompaniment.

It would be agreeable to believe that church music is *ipso facto* divinely inspired, but that unfortunately is not true. If there is inspiration it is an accident, not an inevitable condition. It is the workaday life of service which provides the materials with which composers may or may not achieve the sublime. Purcell at the Chapel Royal and Bach at Leipzig are typical examples of composers who wrote church music because it was needed. By the regular exercise of their craft they had acquired that absolute certainty which is the mark of the professional composer. There was no need to experiment: they knew what they wanted to do. And through this knowledge they were able to rise to heights which are unattainable by those whose desire for self-expression has never been matched by a mastery of their trade. Church music, like opera, is music for a purpose: it is not necessarily, for that reason, a higher or a nobler art. It involves a reconciliation of the claims of edification and'sensuous pleasure. Many composers have been defeated by this problem. They have imagined that edification was sufficient, and that artistry was of minor importance; or else they have sought merely to give pleasure and have forgotten the circumstances in which the music would be performed.

It is also a characteristic of church music that it adheres strongly to tradition, since the liturgy is unchanging and the repertory of the past survives much more vigorously than in the secular field. Hence in societies where church music is highly prized it acts in some measure as a brake on any rapid or sudden change of style. The conservatism of even the most up-to-date composers can be seen in the case of Monteverdi, much of whose church music is in the severest tradition of the sixteenth century. In the modern world church music has had far less influence on the development of music as a whole. There is in consequence a tendency to regard church music as an archaic art. Not only has there been a widespread interest in the music of the past, but also composers have often been inclined to imitate what they admired in such music. Whatever the technical approach, it remains true that truth and sincerity are rooted in belief and cannot be simulated by anyone to whom Christian worship means nothing.

The dual nature of church music—as an intensification of religious experience and as a source of sensuous pleasure—has constantly affected the official attitude towards it. The Christian fathers were often suspicious of the secular associa-

tions of music and particularly of instrumental performance.
Clement of Alexandria (c. 150–220) roundly declares that
music which stirs the emotions should be banished, and he
draws a violent contrast between the devotion proper to
worship and the immorality of secular song. He pictures the
singers leaving the church and forgetting at once where they
have been. Instead of the praises of immortality they now
sing "Let us eat and drink, for tomorrow we die". He adds
grimly: "No, they will not die tomorrow, for they are
already dead before God."[4] A sincere music-lover like St.
Augustine (354–430) could be seriously troubled by the
pleasure he derived from fine singing in the choir:

> When it happens that I am moved more by the music than by
> the words which it accompanies, I confess that I am guilty of a
> grave sin.

His dilemma is all the more embarrassing since he recognizes
that the listener may be more inclined to devotion when the
music is well sung than when it is not.[5]

The use of trained musicians and the increasing elaboration of church music in the Middle Ages gave rise to various
abuses, which were often vigorously condemned. John of
Salisbury (1115–80) says bluntly that "music defiles the
service of religion". He maintains that the simple souls of the
congregation are depraved by the wantonness of the singing
and its womanish affectations. The facility displayed by the
singers is amazing but the performance itself is enervating;
and he vigorously condemns the style of the music sung.[6]
No doubt part of this complaint is directed against the free
improvisations and ornamentation introduced by the
singers; but the nature of the church music of this period
which has survived shows that the composers themselves did
not hesitate to prescribe considerable elaboration. A contemporary of John of Salisbury, Aelred, Abbot of Rievaulx in

Yorkshire (1109–66), speaks in even stronger terms of the extravagance of church music (the translation is from William Prynne's *Histriomastix*, published in 1633):

> Whence hath the Church so many Organs and Musicall Instruments? To what purpose, I pray you, is that terrible blowing of Belloes, expressing rather the crakes of Thunder, than the sweetnesse of a voyce? To what purpose serves that contraction and inflection of the voyce? . . . One while the voyce is strained, anon it is remitted, now it is dashed, and then againe it is inlarged with a lowder sound. Sometimes, which is a shame to speake, it is enforced into a horse's neighings; sometimes, the masculine vigour being laid aside, it is sharpened into the shrilnesse of a woman's voyce; now and then it is writhed, and retorted with a certaine artificiall circumvolution.[7]

Two centuries later Pope John XXII issued from Avignon in 1324 a strong condemnation of the up-to-date church music of his time. He complains of the frequent use of smaller note-values, of the splitting up of melodies with rests, and of the incorporation of secular material in the upper parts of motets. The individual characteristics of the church modes become confused and obscured. The voices intoxicate the ear, and the singers even use gestures to illustrate what they are singing. Devotion is forgotten and licence reigns. The Pope's remedy is the ruthless prohibition of all polyphony as then understood: he allows only the use of consonances— the octave, fifth and fourth.[8] Such a measure was wildly reactionary, and it is not surprising that it was soon ignored, though it may have had the temporary effect of checking extravagance. Historians generally are inclined to believe that its most important result was an increasing cultivation of secular music.

The subject of church music was also one of the matters discussed at the Council of Trent in the sixteenth century. It was decreed in 1562 that any music, whether for organ or for voices, which had any profane elements (*ubi sive organo, sive cantu lascivum aut impurum aliquid miscetur*)[9] should be banished from the church. Nor did the Catholic Church have a monopoly of these protests. In England Robert Browne, in his *True and Short Declaration* (1583), complains bitterly of the antiphonal singing of the psalms and elaborate anthems:

> Their tossing to and fro of psalmes and sentences is like tenisse plaie, whereto God is called to Judg who can do best and be most gallant in his worship: as bie organs, solfaing, pricksong chanting, bussing and mumling verie roundlie, on divers handes. Thus thei have a shewe of religion, but in deed thei turne it to gaming, and plaie mockholidaie with the worship of God[10].

In the following century we find Sir Edward Dering adopting an equally critical attitude to the use of instrumental music at Christ Church, Oxford, where, he observes, "in matter of Religion, they are yet in lov with those specious, pompous, loud, exteriour complements."[11] Bach himself was not immune from criticism. As a young organist at Arnstadt in 1706 he was summoned before the Consistorium to explain why he had been absent for four months without leave and why he had given up the performance of concerted music for voices and instruments; and the opportunity was taken to rebuke him for introducing "curious variations" in his playing of the chorales.[12]

In modern times the most elaborate and thorough statement of the attitude of the Catholic Church has been the *Motu proprio* of Pope Pius X, issued from the Vatican in 1903.[13] Sacred music is defined as "a complementary part of the solemn liturgy": as such "it participates in the general scope of the liturgy, which is the glory of God and the sanctification and edification of the faithful". It must have "sanctity", "goodness of form" and "universality". Gregorian chant is cited as the supreme model of what church music should be: the theatrical style of nineteenth-century church music lies at the farthest extreme from it. Women are excluded from choirs, because the singers have a liturgical office, which women are incapable of exercising. Organ accompaniment is permitted, but the piano and "noisy or frivolous instruments" are forbidden, and the use of wind instruments is allowed only in exceptional circumstances. Finally a plea is made for the restoration of choir schools and for the instruction of theological students in "the principles and laws of sacred music".

The use of instruments in church has always been a stumbling block. They were condemned by the Christian fathers on account of their secular associations but could not be excluded. The pneumatic organ, first used in Constantinople for purely secular purposes, was found convenient for church use on account of its power and its capacity for sustained tone. In the course of the Middle Ages it was developed and improved until it came to be regarded as an indispensable part of the equipment of any cathedral or princely chapel. The unmistakable evidence of pictures and sculpture, however, shows that other instruments were used as well. In the absence of any public concert hall the cathedral was the most suitable place for the performance of large-scale works, and this no doubt encouraged composers in the late sixteenth century towards a more elaborate type of church music in which instruments had independent parts. The splendid compositions of the baroque period are the fulfilment of this type of writing. The practice of writing elaborate Masses with full orchestra continued right down to the nineteenth century and has not yet been abandoned, though such works are not suitable for liturgical use.

One interesting consequence of the use of the organ to support the voices in sixteenth-century church music was the invention of the figured bass. It was originally designed to avoid the labour of providing the organist with a complete score, and also to ensure that the essential harmonies would be heard even if all the voices were not there. But its obvious convenience led to its adoption as the standard form of accompaniment for solo music. From the very beginning of the seventeenth century it was transferred also to secular music, both vocal and instrumental, and for well over 150 years remained the one indispensable element in the performance of music of any kind.

One objection to the use of instruments was that they do not enunciate sacred words, quite apart from their secular associations. The following is a typical appeal to Biblical authority:

I read of Vocal Musick in the New Testament, and Singing of Psalms, but not a word of the little Instrument the Violin; nor the great Bag-pipes, or Organ.[14]

Jeremy Taylor argues more moderately:

The use of Musical instruments may also add some little advantages to singing, but they are more apt to change religion into air and fancies, and take off some of its simplicity, and are not so fitted for edification. *Ad disciplinas aliquid artificiale organum non esse adhibendum*, said *Aristotle* as he is quoted by *Aquinas*. Artificial instruments are not fit to be applied to the use of disciplines. That is, the musick of instruments of it self does not make a man wiser, or instruct him in any thing.[15]

Since Taylor was a High Churchman it is clear that the objection in England to instrumental music in church was not confined to the Puritans. It is true that the Puritans removed a number of organs from cathedrals; but many years earlier in Elizabeth I's reign very strong opposition to the organ had been expressed by the Lower House of Convocation.[16]

In the nineteenth century a curious historical error led to the banning of the organ, on purely aesthetic grounds, from the revival of sixteenth-century church music. The Romantics, in their desire to escape from the present, turned eagerly to the music of this period, delighting in its supposed "purity" and remoteness from the turbulence of their own time. Believing that such music was always performed unaccompanied, they established the tradition that *a cappella* (in the church style) meant "without instruments"— a tradition which is still vigorous at the present day. No one can deny that the church music of the sixteenth century can sound exquisite on voices alone; but there is no justification whatever for asserting that it was always so performed. There is, in fact, direct evidence to the contrary—for example, in the organ scores of Elizabethan church music. The Romantics also rediscovered Bach—largely through Mendelssohn's pioneer work in performing the *St. Matthew Passion*. In their enthusiasm they did not always understand him, and they were apt to see in his music romantic elements which answered to their own aspirations. A practical result, however, was the composition of a number of works for chorus and orchestra, written, like Bach's cantatas, for the Protestant Church. At the other extreme was the desire for festival compositions on a grand scale, which had its origin in the celebrations organized in Paris at the time of the Revolution (see p. 91). The tradition of pagan magnificence survived till the Empire and was suitably adapted to the needs of religion. Berlioz's *Messe des morts* and *Te Deum* are the best-known examples of this practice.

[1] P. Wagner, *Introduction to the Gregorian Melodies*, I (London, 1907), p. 19.
[2] Ibid., p. 24.
[3] A. W. Haddan and W. Stubbs, *Councils and Ecclesiastical Documents*, vol. iii (Oxford, 1871), p. 367; translation in G. Reese, *Music in the Middle Ages* (New York, 1940), p. 133. Clovesho appears to have been somewhere in Kent, though its exact location is unknown.
[4] Th. Gérold, *Les Pères de l'Église et la musique* (Paris, 1931), p. 96.
[5] Ibid., p. 105.
[6] The passage is translated in *The Oxford History of Music*, vol. i, 2nd ed. (London, 1929), p. 290, n. 1.

[7] Quoted in Percy A. Scholes, *The Puritans and Music* (London, 1934), p. 215.

[8] For the complete passage see *The Oxford History of Music*, vol. i, 2nd ed. (London, 1929), pp. 294–6.

[9] H. Coates, *Palestrina* (London, 1938), p. 12, n. 1.

[10] Quoted in Scholes, op. cit., p. 217.

[11] Joseph Brookbank, *The Well-tuned Organ* (London, 1660), p. 51.

[12] Hans T. David and Arthur Mendel, *The Bach Reader*, 2nd ed. (New York, 1966), pp. 51–2.

[13] Complete English translation in N. Slonimsky, *Music since 1900*, 4th ed. (New York, 1971), pp. 1285–9.

[14] Edmund Hickeringill, *The Ceremony-Monger, His Character* (London, 1689), p. 34.

[15] *Ductor Dubitantium, or the Rule of Conscience*, 3rd ed. (London 1676), p. 670.

[16] On this subject see further Scholes, op. cit., chap. xv.

CHAPTER VI

PATRONAGE

THE influence of the Church may be said to have been one-sided, since it has primarily been concerned with music written for a liturgical purpose, though it may indirectly have affected secular music as well. The connexion of the State with music is more far-reaching. We may consider first its activity as a patron, and secondly the effect of such patronage on composition. State patronage is naturally linked with the history of church music, since kings and emperors maintained large chapels, where the music might be as elaborate as in any cathedral. A fifteenth-century poet expresses strong enthusiasm for the chapel of Henry V of England, who was himself a composer:

> Psallit plena Deo cantoribus ampla capella,
> Carmine sidereo laudabilis est ea cella.[1]

(An abundant chapel, filled with singers, makes music to God,
It is a building which deserves praise for its heavenly song.)

Such patronage was the support of many eminent musicians. Paul Hofhaimer and Heinrich Isaac in the late fifteenth century owed their maintenance to the Emperor Maximilian I. The splendid church music heard at Versailles in the seventeenth century not only glorified God but was testimony also to the magnificence of Louis XIV. Such maintenance was not confined to royalty. The church music of Heinrich Schütz was written for the chapel of the Elector of Saxony at Dresden, and Monteverdi was *maestro di cappella della serenissima republica di Venetia* (choirmaster of the most noble

88

Republic of Venice). In this environment many promising musicians were reared: Purcell was a choirboy in the English Chapel Royal, Schubert a court chorister in Vienna.

Musicians employed by the State formed part of the official retinue of the ruler. In addition to the singers in the chapel there were also trumpeters and drummers, who were originally used only for military and ceremonial purposes but became absorbed into the orchestra in the seventeenth century, and a number of instrumentalists whose function was to provide entertainment and to supplement the voices in the chapel. There might also be a body of singers whose duties were confined to secular music. The scale of such establishments was larger than was normally possible under private patronage. Their origin is to be found in the bodies of minstrels employed in medieval courts. In course of time they became more highly organized, and this helped to make possible the creation of the orchestra in the seventeenth century. The best string-players in France were employed in Louis XIV's *vingt-quatre violons du Roi* (the King's twenty-four violins[2])—an organization which was exactly copied in England by Charles II's "four and twenty fiddlers". Eighteenth-century orchestras also were normally maintained by rulers, though there are certain exceptions—for example, the *Concert spirituel* in Paris, the players employed by Handel in London for his operas and oratorios, and the concerts organized there for Haydn by Johann Peter Salomon. In addition, opera was frequently a court function or was supported by royalty. In the early nineteenth century the picture begins to change. We see the growth of a wider public for music, and in consequence the formation of societies to provide orchestral concerts by subscription: typical examples are the Gesellschaft der Musikfreunde (Society of Friends of Music) in Vienna, founded in 1813, and the Philharmonic Society (now the Royal Philharmonic Society) in London, which dates from the same year. These developments were partly the result of the social and political changes which followed the French Revolution. They did not immediately put an end to State patronage; but they pointed the way to the modern system of institutions which are artistically, if not economically, independent.

Individual musicians, however much their talents were admired and however much we may revere them from a distance, were regarded simply as part of the equipment of a court. Lassus, Lully and C. P. E. Bach were the employees respectively of the Duke of Bavaria, Louis XIV and Frederick the Great: as such they had specific duties to perform. Outstanding merit might, of course, be marked by signs of favour. Lassus, for example, was ennobled by Maximilian II, and Frederick the Great gave a warm and enthusiastic welcome to J. S. Bach when he paid a visit to his son at Potsdam. "Gentlemen," he exclaimed to his musicians, "old Bach is come"; and he laid aside his flute to receive the visitor. We read further how Bach was invited to try the king's pianos and improvised the fugue which stands at the beginning of the *Musikalisches Opfer*.[3] Handel in England, though not dependent on patronage for his livelihood, owed much to the support and encouragement of George II. Perhaps the most extravagant example of royal favour is to be found in the relations between Ludwig II of Bavaria and Wagner. The king writes ecstatically:

I can only adore you, only praise the power that led you to me. More clearly and ever more clearly do I feel that I cannot reward you as you deserve: all I do, all I can ever do for you, can be no better than stammered thanks. An earthly being cannot requite a divine spirit. But it can love, it can venerate: you are my first, my only love, and ever will be.[4]

Beside such enthusiasm Queen Victoria's amiable interest in Mendelssohn is like milk and water.

It is not until the very end of the eighteenth century that

we find the State taking an interest in composers as artists, rather than as employees. This development was in some measure due to the French Revolution. Both during and after the Revolution music was in considerable demand for public ceremonies, and composers were frequently commissioned to write works for these occasions. It is true that one of the objects of such music was to glorify the régime, but there was at the same time a realization that the arts were worthy of honour in their own right, and the composers who contributed music were by no means subservient nonentities. One of the most important was Gossec, who was born in the Netherlands but spent most of his life in Paris. Having already established his reputation as a composer before the Revolution, he found no difficulty in adapting himself to the new order and wrote many works for public occasions, including music for the funeral of Mirabeau, "in which", in the words of Grove's *Dictionary*, "he introduced the lugubrious sounds of the gong". These performances, which were on a grandiose scale and demanded a large number of participants, established a tradition which was maintained under the Empire and the restoration of the monarchy and survived the Revolution of 1830. Berlioz's *Messe des morts* and *Symphonie funèbre et triomphale*, both of which were originally designed to commemorate anniversaries of the 1830 Revolution, are late examples of this monumental style.

A further consequence of the French Revolution was the establishment by the Convention Nationale in 1795 of the Conservatoire National de Musique, a successor of the École Royale de Chant founded in 1784. The initiative had been taken by the members of the band of the Garde Nationale, and the original plan of the Conservatoire was that it should reunite a body of expert musicians who would be able to take part in celebrations of the *fêtes nationales* and at the same time give free instruction in all branches of music to 600 pupils, chosen from all the departments of France.

The latter purpose, which shows an unusually enlightened attitude to the arts, has survived. Direct support for composers, as opposed to students, has never been common. Finland, however, has given annual grants to a number of composers, beginning with Sibelius, though these have not apparently been large enough to relieve the recipients of all financial responsibility.[5] The case of Soviet Russia is rather different. There composers receive substantial support from the State, with subsidies for medical treatment and holidays; but this is in a sense payment for services rendered, since the musicians are expected to write the kind of music that is approved by the Government and to avoid any contamination from bourgeois influences.[6]

State patronage has had various effects on music. The most obvious has been the composition of works for State or official occasions, such as the Agincourt song in the fifteenth century, the royal odes written by Purcell and other composers in Restoration England, and the settings of the *Te Deum* which have often been written to celebrate a victory or the end of a conflict. Since the State has generally been able to offer more generous rewards than private patrons, musicians have at all periods been anxious to ingratiate themselves with the authorities and to win official recognition. The Kyrie and Gloria of Bach's Mass in B minor were written in 1733 with the express purpose of securing a court title from Frederick Augustus II, Elector of Saxony and subsequently King of Poland. "For some years and up to the present moment," he writes in the letter accompanying the music,

I have had the *Directorium* of the Music in the two principal churches in Leipzig, but have innocently had to suffer one injury or another, and on occasion also a diminution of the fees accruing to me in this office; but these injuries would disappear altogether if Your Royal Highness would grant me the favour of conferring upon me a title of Your Highness's Court Capelle, and would let Your High Command for the issuing of such a document go forth to the proper place.[7]

Purcell, in 1683, dedicating his trio sonatas to Charles II, makes bold to lay his compositions at his Majesty's "Sacred feet", observing that "they are the immediate Results of your Majesties Royall favour, and benignity to me which have made me what I am". Such language, which may appear uncomfortably obsequious to readers of a later age, is nothing more than the natural expression of polite respect to a ruler on whom the musician depends for his livelihood. Royalty not only held the purse-strings of court appointments. Individuals might also receive particular favours. We have seen already how Tallis and Byrd in 1575 were granted a monopoly of music-printing by Elizabeth I—a monopoly which included the importing of foreign publications and the selling of music-paper.[8] Louis XIV showed his interest in opera in a practical way by granting the poet Pierre Perrin a patent, dated 1669, for the sole representation of such works in France.[9] The advantages to be derived from such patronage did not prevent some composers from showing independence. Handel and Wagner both owed something to royal favour; but they were both too individual-ist to rely on it for their livelihood, and both of them made their mark by the persistence with which they carved out a career for themselves. Even more striking is the case of Beethoven, who never held any official appointment once he had left Bonn for Vienna.

In most cases State patronage has been responsible for providing financial support without giving any particular direction to composers. There have, however, been cases of rulers whose personal interest in music was sufficiently strong to influence local developments. An example in the late eighteenth century is the Emperor Joseph II, who believed fervently in the establishment in Vienna of a national German opera. The movement to which he gave his encouragement was short-lived, but we owe to it the composition of Mozart's *Die Entführung*. Very different is the ideology which has been imposed on Russian music in the last thirty years. The Russian Association of Proletarian Musicians was dissolved in 1932; but its programme, as formulated in 1929, remains very close to the ideals pursued by the Soviet Government today. It condemns bourgeois music as "decadent" and represents the members of the Association as striving "to reflect the rich, full-blooded psychology of the proletariat, as historically the most advanced, and dialectically the most sensitive and understanding class".[10]

In general, State patronage may be said to have been responsible for maintaining traditions and for providing composers with opportunities for the practice of their craft. It has also, through dynastic marriages, contributed to the spread of international culture and to the adoption of foreign fashions. Inevitably it has restricted the cultivation and appreciation of music to a small minority of the population who were connected with the Court or could afford to maintain establishments of their own. The spread of music among a larger public does not occur until the nineteenth century and is an indirect result of the final breakdown of feudalism in Europe. The traditions established by State patronage, however, survived the old order. Nowhere is that more evident than in Germany. Through the existence of a large number of individual states opera was cultivated on an extensive scale. The kings and princes who maintained them have long since disappeared, but modern Germany can still claim the existence of more opera-houses than any other country in the world. In Italy there has been a similar, though more modest, inheritance of political conditions which are now obsolete.

The employment of musicians by private persons is in some measure a reflection of State patronage. Its origin is no doubt to be found in the practice of employing slave musicians under the Roman Empire. The medieval descendant of the slave musician was the itinerant minstrel, who depended for his livelihood not merely on the casual patronage of those he visited but often on a permanent situation in one of the noble households. The name *jongleur*, derived from the Latin *ioculator* (from which comes also the English "juggler"), shows clearly enough the nature of his employment. In addition to his skill as a musician he was often able to offer entertainment of a more general kind. He was conjurer, acrobat, musician and music-hall artist in one. The more skilful musicians could count on the support of the troubadours, who needed them for the performance of their songs. The troubadours, however, were not only patrons: some of them rose from a humble origin and were themselves, in the first place, the object of patronage. One of the most famous of the Provençal troubadours, Bernard de Ventadour, who died in 1195, took his name from the castle of Ventadour, where his mother had been in charge of the bakery fire.[11]

Feudalism encouraged the growth of musical establishments, and many of these survived in later ages, in spite of the competition of State patronage. Ambition and wealth were a powerful incentive to the imitation of royal splendour. The passionate desire of German princes to copy Louis XIV's court at Versailles is typical of the snobbery to which many musicians owed their employment. It was satirized superbly by La Fontaine in his fable of the frog that wished to be as big as an ox, ending with the acid comment:

> Le monde est plein de gens qui ne sont pas plus sages:
> Tout bourgeois veut bâtir comme les grands seigneurs;
> Tout petit prince a des ambassadeurs;
> Tout marquis veut avoir des pages.

The result of such employment was not necessarily servitude. In a genuinely artistic society friendly relations were possible between the aristocracy and mere musicians. This was the case in fourteenth-century Italy, when the blind organist Landini was held in high honour by the rich Alberti family.[12] Italy was for centuries a fruitful soil for music. Here flourished a number of small dukedoms and principalities, and here also arose a mercantile aristocracy which did not despise the arts. It was only natural that in these favourable conditions musicians and patrons should meet on equal terms.

It was in such a society that opera came to birth in Florence at the end of the sixteenth century, when Peri's *Dafne* was performed privately at Jacopo Corsi's house; and its most famous successor, Monteverdi's *Orfeo*, also enjoyed a private performance before the Accademia degl' invaghiti at Mantua in 1607. In this world—a world which took equal delight in poetry and in music—the madrigal developed into a subtle and delicate form of musical expression. Those for whose pleasure it was designed were willing patrons, and we need not suppose that the dedications in which composers acknowledged their interest were merely conventional expressions of gratitude. When styles changed and the solo cantata became fashionable in the early seventeenth century the social setting was the same. Music was not merely honoured; it was understood. We find rather similar conditions in England. John Wilbye's patrons, the Kytson family of Hengrave Hall in Suffolk, were clearly people of considerable culture, for whom music was something more than a fashionable pastime. We need not suppose that music was universally appreciated. Wilbye, dedicating his second book of madrigals (1609) to Arabella Stuart, declared that "Musicke sits solitary among her sister Sciences, and . . . often wants the fortune to be esteemed (for so she is worthy) even among the worthyest". But since he was fortunate in his patrons he cannot have had any serious cause for complaint. The dedications of the English collections of lute-songs show an equal indebtedness to patrons. As Robert Jones puts it in the dedication of his *Second Booke of Song and Ayres* (1601):

We have no way to heighten our being but by another power. As gentlewomen peise [i.e. burden] themselves with tires and coronets, to appear more personable and tall, so must we add unto our littleness (if we will not be scorned for dwarfs) the crown of gentle persons more eminent and high.

Patronage was for the most part an individual matter. There was, however, an unusual example of co-operation in London at the end of the seventeenth century, when "several persons of quality" offered four prizes, totalling 200 guineas, for a composition. The prizes were won respectively by John Weldon, John Eccles, Daniel Purcell and Godfrey Finger. The awards caused some dissatisfaction, since the persons of quality themselves acted as judges, instead of calling in experts. Roger North observes:

The Lords & the rest that subscribed . . . had ears, but not artificiall ones, and those were necessary to warrant the authority of such a court of justice.[13]

Finger, a German by birth, was so disgusted that he left the country, "declaring that he thought he was to compose musick for men, and not for boys".

Even so independent a character as Handel enjoyed the favour of patrons when he first came to England. According to Hawkins[14] he

began to yield to the invitations of such persons of rank and fortune as were desirous of his acquaintance, and accepted an invitation from one Mr. Andrews, of Barn-Elms, in Surrey, but who had also a town residence, to apartments in his house.

D

Nothing is known of Mr. Andrews, but we are better informed about the Earl of Burlington, in whose house in Piccadilly Handel was, if not a permanent resident, at least a constant visitor during the years 1715–18. Gay, in his poem *Trivia* (1716), describes Burlington House as "belov'd by ev'ry Muse" and gives a vivid picture of Handel performing there.[15] The exact nature of Handel's association with the Duke of Chandos is not known: there is no evidence that he actually resided in the luxurious mansion at Cannons. But it seems reasonably certain that we owe to this association the Chandos *Te Deum*, the Chandos anthems, *Haman and Mordecai* (the first version of the oratorio *Esther*), and *Acis and Galatea*. Bach's livelihood was ensured by permanent employment; but the interest of a patron was responsible for the composition of the six orchestral works which we know as the Brandenburg concertos. The composer's dedication to the Markgraf of Brandenburg, written, according to the fashion of the times, in French, expresses the great pleasure which he had in fulfilling the patron's request. He humbly begs the prince

not to judge their imperfection with the rigour of the fine and delicate taste which the whole world knows Your Highness has for musical pieces; but rather to infer from them in benign Consideration the profound respect and the most humble obedience which I try to show Your Highness therewith.[16]

It seems doubtful, however, whether the Markgraf appreciated the honour which Bach had done him. The concertos were not mentioned in the catalogue of his library, and the score was merely included in a miscellaneous collection of manuscripts which were sold after his death in 1734.[17]

The outstanding example of patronage in the second half of the eighteenth century is Haydn's long period of service with the Esterházy family. He was appointed Vice-*Kapell-*

meister (or deputy director of music) in 1761 at the age of twenty-nine, became *Kapellmeister* five years later, and retired with a pension in 1790. The conditions of his appointment have been preserved.[18] They make it clear that he is to be "considered and treated as a member of the household". He is to treat the musicians with due consideration and to see that both he and they wear the proper uniform when they are summoned to perform. His own conduct must be exemplary, and he is reminded of the importance of punctuality, proper charge of the instruments and music, and his obligation to compose such music as his employer may demand. These conditions, though framed in agreeable terms, might seem very much like servitude to a modern musician, particularly the prohibition against writing music for any other person without the Prince's permission. Haydn's own comment was characteristic: "I was cut off from the world. There was no one to confuse or torment me, and I was forced to become original." There can, in fact, be no doubt that his extraordinary mastery of the orchestra was the product of these long years of practical experience. The basis of originality cannot be so easily established; but Haydn may very well have been right in suggesting that this secluded life helped him to find himself as a composer. After his retirement he wrote to his friend Maria von Genzinger:

How sweet is some degree of liberty! I had a kind Prince, but was obliged at times to be dependent on base souls. I often sighed for release and now I have it in some measure.[19]

This would suggest that his employment had its drawbacks; but however much he may have fretted under the material conditions of his work, the opportunities which it offered must have outweighed the disadvantages.

Mozart's temperament was not suited to this kind of employment. He found service with the Archbishop at

Salzburg intolerable. For the same reason he found it difficult to secure the intermittent patronage which so many of his contemporaries enjoyed. He was, however, quite ready to write anything for anyone if he could be certain of a performance—or even simply for the promise of a fee. As a young man in Paris he conquered his dislike of the flute and harp sufficiently to write a concerto for these two instruments (K.299) for the Duc de Guines, though he had the greatest difficulty in getting paid for it. The Duke was equally unreliable in the matter of his daughter's lessons in composition, which was all the more galling since the girl had no ideas whatever and must have been an exasperating pupil.[20]

Beethoven professed a profound contempt for the aristocracy. He told Goethe at Teplitz what happened when he was asked to give lessons to Duke Rainer:

> He let me wait in the antechamber, and for that I gave his fingers a good twisting; when he asked me why I was so impatient I said that he had wasted my time in the anteroom and I could wait no longer with patience. After that he never let me wait again.

When the Empress and the royal dukes approached, he shocked Goethe by refusing to make way for them.[21] In spite of this display of bad manners he was on friendly terms with many persons of noble birth. The dedications of his piano sonatas are a permanent record of these associations. Three noblemen—Archduke Rudolph, Prince Lobkowitz and Prince Kinsky—combined to guarantee him an annual grant of 4,000 gulden on condition that he declined the invitation of Jerome Bonaparte, King of Westphalia, to become his *Kapellmeister* at Kassel.[22] He was quite happy to receive their support, but he would have been horrified at the suggestion that they were his patrons: he regarded himself as their equals. By thus combining idealism with common sense he made the best of both worlds.

Such an attitude would have been impossible for
Schubert, not only because the circumstances of his upbringing gave him no opportunity for mixing with the aristocracy, but also because by temperament he was more at
home in the happy-go-lucky society of his friends. His
experience of patronage was brief. For two short periods, in
1818 and 1824, he taught the daughters of Count Esterházy
at Zseliz in Hungary, but the experience seems to have made
little impression on him. His comments on his first visit are
mainly confined to his fellow-servants, whom he seems to
have found mostly agreeable, though the two grooms were
"more fit for traffic with horses than with human beings".[23]

A rather different kind of patronage was enjoyed by John
Field, the Irish pianist and composer. He was apprenticed to
Clementi in London and employed by him to demonstrate
the qualities of pianos for sale in his music shop. This might
strictly be described as a commercial situation rather than
patronage. However, Field had the advantage of receiving
piano lessons from his employer, and of travelling with him
to the Continent. Spohr met the two of them in St. Petersburg and was strongly impressed by the young man (see
p. 36), though the lack of a common language was a barrier
to any thorough acquaintanceship. He recalls too how he
found Clementi and his pupil doing their own washing,
because it was cheaper than the laundry.[24]

Both Liszt and Chopin would have found such a situation
highly undignified, if not actually inconceivable. Both of
them were lionized by Society and so enjoyed the benefits of
patronage without owing allegiance to any individual.
Chopin himself seems to have been innocently surprised by
his success in Paris. "I have gained the entrée to the first
circles," he writes in 1833; "I have my place among ambas-
sadors, princes, ministers, but I really don't know by what
miracle it has happened".[25] Liszt would never have considered it a miracle: he accepted conquest as an unchallenged

right. It is to his credit that the adulation he received did not prevent him from offering encouragement to others. His twelve years as director of the Court music at Weimar were marked by a generosity to other musicians which is one of the most admirable traits in his character. In his earlier years in Paris he had protested vigorously against the situation of inferiority to which artists were often condemned in contemporary society, "against the oppressive iniquity or the insolent stupidity that blights and tortures them and condescends merely to use them as playthings".[26] The crumbling of the older system of private patronage had produced a state of affairs in which, though a few outstanding musicians might be the darlings of Society, the majority were little more than hired entertainers. Max von Weber, son of the composer, comments acidly on the treatment received by a musician in an aristocratic London household at this time:

He performed, was paid, and then had to leave without being regarded as one of the guests of the house. The insolent lackeys served him differently from the "guests", and would have blushed at the idea of offering him refreshments in the drawing room. His host greeted him condescendingly and pointed out to him his place, which, in many salons, was separated by a cord from that of the guests.[27]

Liszt's protest was not, like Beethoven's rudeness, a mere expression of individual pride: it was a plea for a new social order, in which artists, irrespective of their birth or origin, should be valued for themselves and for the contribution they made to the welfare of mankind.

In the course of the nineteenth century private patronage in the old sense became increasingly rare. When it occurred it was inevitably a sign of wealth; but it might also be an indication of eccentricity. Madame von Meck was very generous to Tchaikovsky, but it is doubtful whether so emotional a relationship was good for him; even though she made it a condition that they should never meet. She could write to him:

Your march, Peter Ilyich, is so beautiful that it lifts me, as I had hoped, into that mood of blissful madness in which one can forget all that is bitter and offensive in the world. It is impossible to describe the chaos that reigns in my head and heart when I hear it. A shiver runs through my nerves—I want to sob, to die, I long for another life, but not the life that others believe in and look forward to, a life that is different, intangible, indescribable.[28]

This is dangerously near hysteria. In most modern examples of patronage there is probably some element of selfish satisfaction. No one questions the help which Lord Howard de Walden gave to Joseph Holbrooke, but no one can help regretting that the composer was saddled with the impossible librettos written by his patron under the name T. E. Ellis. None the less there have been examples of enlightened and disinterested patronage in the present century—for example, the encouragement given to composers of chamber music by W. W. Cobbett in England and Elizabeth Sprague Coolidge in America, and the splendid benefactions of George Eastman at Rochester (N.Y.). But the conditions of modern life have made it increasingly more difficult for individuals to endow the arts. More and more the responsibility for commissioning new works, securing publication, and maintaining orchestras has been assumed by public bodies such as the Carnegie Trust, the B.B.C., the Arts Council and municipal corporations.

The whole question of patronage is intimately bound up with the economics of music—a subject which no musician can afford to ignore. Under a system of patronage composers and performers may be entirely dependent on the wealth and whims of an individual. The pages of history are full of complaints from those whose position made them employees. An anonymous satire on the Emperor Rudolph I (1218–91) praises the ruler for his kingly virtues and honourable acts but observes that he gives no rewards to his musicians:

> Der meister syngen, gigen, sagen;
> Daz hort her gern und git yn drummé nicht.[29]

If we need a later example we have only to turn to a letter written by Monteverdi to the Secretary of State at Mantua in 1608 (the year of *Arianna*), in which he protests that he is badly paid and grossly overworked.[30] Employment might even, paradoxically, be an obstacle to money-making. A petition of Tallis and Byrd to Elizabeth I in 1577 explains that the former has had no preferment after forty years' service and the latter, having had to move from Lincoln Cathedral to the Chapel Royal, is in serious financial straits, since his daily duties prevent him from making an income from teaching. The petition also points out that the monopoly of printing which they received two years earlier (see p. 93) has been no source of profit but has in fact worked out at a loss.[31] Such complaints have sometimes involved elaborate controversy. Bach's dispute over fees with the University of Leipzig lasted two years and was eventually carried to the King-Elector.[32]

A rise in the cost of living has naturally been one of the grievances of musicians. An entry in the Cheque Book of the English Chapel Royal, dated 1604, gratefully records an increase of stipend made by James I from £30 to £40 per annum for each gentleman of the chapel. But by the time of Charles II it was claimed that the cost of living had risen by more than a hundred per cent, and in 1662 there was a further increase to £70.[33] There was always, however, a danger that salaries would be in arrears. When Charles I's wind players were summoned to attend him at York in 1642 they declared themselves very willing to obey but protested that since their salaries were two years in arrears they and their families were destitute and they were quite unable to make the journey.[34] Under Charles II the arrears were so serious that many of the musicians were near starvation. Pepys tells of a harpist in the royal service, named Lewis Evans, who did in fact "die for mere want, and was fain to be buried at the almes of the parish".[35] More serious still was the effect of any disruption of official employment. The Civil War in England threw a great number of skilled musicians out of work. Some of them were successful in securing private patrons during the Commonwealth; others had to live by their wits.

So long as patronage was the normal system of employment for a musician anyone who declined to accept it or was unable to secure it had to rely on his own enterprise, as a virtuoso or as an impresario. Skill was not necessarily an immediate passport to fame. Roger North relates how the Italian violinist, Nicola Matteis, played wonderfully when he came to England in the reign of Charles II but because he set too high a value on his achievements was slow in winning recognition. Some friends, however, showed him "the temper of the English, who if they were humoured, would be liberall, but if not humoured would doe nothing at all"; and profiting by their advice he gained many pupils and persuaded them and others to buy his compositions, "which brought him the 3, 4, and 5 ginnys".[36] Mozart's career as an infant prodigy shows how industriously a travelling musician was forced to work if his journey was to be profitable. It is possible to understand, if not to forgive, Leopold Mozart's ambition to exploit his son; but it remains true that this was not the best way of educating a precocious and sensitive child. Individual enterprise was at all times precarious and might easily end in disaster. In 1761 the *Public Advertiser* in London published an affecting petition from the Italian *castrato* Ferdinando Tenducci, who had been imprisoned because he was unable to satisfy his creditors in Italy:

> Being destitute of Friends, and reduced to the utmost Indigence and Misery, he begs Leave to fly to the distinguished Benevolence of the Nobility and Gentry of this Kingdom, imploring their Compassion towards an unfortunate Stranger in Distress, and intreating the Honour of their Company at the Great Music-Room in Dean-street, Soho, where, on Wednesday, the 28th of January 1761, some of the best Professors of Music will generously perform for his Benefit.[37]

It is a measure of Handel's practical ability as an impresario that he never reached this extremity. It is true that in the course of his operatic enterprises he lost money heavily (though he was never actually bankrupt). But during his last season he made £1,950 by his oratorios, and he died worth £20,000. His numerous bequests included £2,000 to his amanuensis Christopher Smith and £1,000 to the Society for the Support of Decayed Musicians and their Families.[38] If we take into account the change in the value of money since the eighteenth century, it is evident that Handel was a highly successful man. This cannot be said of Mozart, who throughout his adult life showed an extraordinary incapacity for organizing his affairs, combined with an unfortunate truculence towards those who were in a position to offer him employment. The despairing letters addressed to his friend and brother freemason Michael Puchberg in the last years of his life are a melancholy commentary on the straits to which a genius could be reduced. Like everyone else in a similar position he is full of optimism for the future: it is just at the moment that he is in desperate circumstances and badly in need of help. The embarrassment with which he asks for money is matched only by the misery of his situation. Puchberg proved a true friend, though he may well have guessed that there would be further requests for money.

Perhaps the most pathetic detail in these distressing letters is a postscript (dated 17th May, 1790) which says:

I now have two pupils and should very much like to raise the number to eight. Do your best to spread the news that I am willing to give lessons.[39]

Beethoven, careless and unpractical though he was in many ways, was too shrewd in money matters to land himself in any such embarrassment. His relations with his publishers —particularly over the *Missa Solennis*—may be regarded, according to the point of view, as good business or doubtful morality. Whatever view we take, there is no doubt that he knew perfectly well how to look after himself. Even Schubert, who never had any permanent employment and had no influential acquaintances, managed to support himself without ever relapsing into hopeless penury. He was largely dependent on the generosity of his friends, on the income from his published works and on casual employment such as accompanying. In addition he once gave a concert of his own compositions. These resources were not abundant, but it is estimated that he made £760 over a period of twelve years. This was worth about £2,000 in 1925 and would be worth considerably more at the present day.[40] The sum does not represent a princely income, but for a bachelor it was an appreciable distance from beggary. Schubert's relations with his publishers were more naïve than Beethoven's. We find him in 1826 writing almost identical letters to two Leipzig publishing firms—Probst and Breitkopf & Härtel— offering them his compositions, including the octet.[41] But it would never have occurred to him to play off one against the other.

Nineteenth-century composers often found their independence a mixed blessing. Without regular employment it was not easy for anyone with any originality to make a living by writing music. Berlioz, like many other French composers since his time, solved the problem by writing musical criticism; but he chafed under the irksome necessity, all the more since it took up time which he would have preferred to devote to composition. He tells a vivid story of the temptation which once came to him to write a symphony. He had heard the work in a dream, and on waking could remember most of the first movement. He was on the point of writing it down when he reflected that once he began he would have to write the whole work. It would probably be a very long work, and might take three or four months' continuous work. He would have no time to write for the press, and his income would diminish accordingly. When the work was finished he would have it copied and performed, and in the process would lose more money. He would have nothing left to support his sick wife and his son. Faced with these reflections he decided to do nothing. The following night the symphony appeared again in his dream, but once more prudence prevailed in his waking hours, and the next day he had forgotten the music completely.[42]

This problem has continued to exercise composers. One solution is to write works to order; but the number of works specially commissioned is now few, and no one could make a livelihood from this alone. Another way out of the difficulty is to write popular music—pot-boilers, in fact—and, if shame forbids acknowledgement of their authorship, to publish them under a pseudonym, much as literary men often make their living by writing detective stories under assumed names. This has the advantage of keeping the hand in practice, but in the long run is liable to be as irksome as writing musical criticism, unless the monetary reward is so alluring as to divert the composer wholly into this type of work. It is also difficult to do successfully, since even popular music must be the product of sincerity, and a composer who writes with his tongue in his cheek or simply to make money is not likely to produce anything convincing. One exceptional means of making money was discovered by Strauss in his old age, when the war had left him in serious straits: he made copies of his orchestral works and sold them to Americans, who could legitimately claim that they had bought an autograph, even if there were half a dozen of the same work. The condition of success in this cold-blooded commercialism was, of course, that the composer was already famous, since no one would have bothered to purchase the autographs of a nobody.

The maintenance of music, like the livelihood of individual musicians, has often in the past depended on a patron's fancy. Large establishments were not simply the result of enthusiasm for music: they were often the product of a desire to astonish the world by the greatest possible magnificence. Where this desire was modest, or the means to fulfil it were lacking, we find an equally modest provision for music. The records of eighteenth-century orchestras[43] include many that are not remarkable for size and were probably not very remarkable for artistry. The system did, however, provide permanent employment for a large number of musicians, since the orchestras were numerous, even if their membership was often small.

The decay of patronage created serious problems for orchestral music, just at the time when it was beginning to reach a wider public. The formation of an orchestra into a society, governed by a committee, either of its own members or of independent persons, does not solve these problems: indeed it creates others, since any independent management has to balance the solvency of the organization against the players' demand for a living wage. We are beginning to realize today the extent to which music in the past has been dependent on the generosity of individuals, who were always ready to put their hands in their pockets when the need arose. The spacious days of the English festivals are largely over, not because we have lost interest in festivals as such, but simply because there has been a drastic reduction in the purchasing power of the community, and in particular in the number of people rich enough and interested enough to keep music alive for its own sake. The logical conclusion, already widely though not universally adopted, is that music needs to be subsidized from public funds, exactly as museums, picture galleries and libraries are subsidized. The objections to such a system, and the dangers to which it is exposed, are the same in each case. The objection that only a small proportion of the community benefits from such a subsidy need not be seriously considered, since the arts do not fall into the same category as public transport, medical treatment or the necessities of daily life. More serious are the dangers inherent in the system. So long as a subsidy is independent of any artistic control it fulfils its purpose admirably; but once the holders of the purse-strings begin to dictate to performers and composers, the system defeats its own end and art becomes merely the servant of politics.

[1] C. A. Cole, *Memorials of Henry V, King of England* (London, 1858) p. 68.
[2] "Violin" is here a generic term, including the larger members of the violin family.
[3] Hans T. David and Arthur Mendel, *The Bach Reader*, 2nd ed. (New York, 1966), pp. 176, 305–6.
[4] Ernest Newman, *The Life of Richard Wagner*, vol. iii (London, 1945), pp. 239–40.
[5] K. Ekman, *Jean Sibelius* (London, 1936), pp. 120–3.
[6] G. Abraham, *Eight Soviet Composers* (London, 1943), pp. 7–12.
[7] Hans T. David and Arthur Mendel, *The Bach Reader*, 2nd ed. (New York, 1966), p. 128.
[8] E. H. Fellowes, *William Byrd*, 2nd ed. (London, 1948), pp. 7–8.
[9] J. Combarieu, *Histoire de la musique*, vol. ii (2nd ed., Paris, 1920), pp. 80–1.
[10] N. Slonimsky, *Music since 1900*, 4th ed. (New York, 1971), p. 1357.
[11] P. Aubry, *Trouvères et troubadours*, 2nd ed. (Paris, 1910), p. 119.
[12] Leonard Ellinwood, *The Works of Francesco Landini* (Cambridge, Mass., 1939), p. xv.
[13] *Roger North on Music*, ed. John Wilson (London, 1959), p. 354. "Artificial" = "expert".
[14] *A General History of the Science and Practice of Music* (1875 ed.), vol. ii, p. 859.
[15] W. C. Smith, *Concerning Handel* (London, 1948), pp. 42–3.

[16] Hans T. David and Arthur Mendel, *The Bach Reader*, 2nd ed. (New York, 1966), pp. 82–3.

[17] C. S. Terry, *Bach: a Biography*, 2nd ed. (London, 1933), p. 135.

[18] A complete translation is printed in J. C. Hadden, *Haydn*, 2nd ed. (London, 1934), pp. 36–9, and Karl Geiringer, *Haydn: a Creative Life in Music*, 2nd ed. (London 1964), pp. 45–7.

[19] Hadden, op. cit., p. 216.

[20] Emily Anderson, *The Letters of Mozart and his Family*, 2nd ed. (London, 1966), pp. 538, 586–7, 716–17.

[21] *Beethoven: Impressions of Contemporaries* (New York, 1927), p. 87.

[22] A. W. Thayer, *The Life of Ludwig van Beethoven*, ed. Elliot Forbes (Princeton, 1964), p. 457.

[23] Otto Erich Deutsch, *Schubert: a Documentary Biography* (London, 1946), pp. 99–100.

[24] *Louis Spohr's Autobiography* (London, 1865), vol. i, pp. 39–40.

[25] Arthur Hedley, *Chopin* (London, 1947), p. 53.

[26] Ernest Newman, *The Life of Richard Wagner*, vol. i (London, 1933), p. 165.

[27] Ibid., p. 158.

[28] Catherine Drinker Bowen and Barbara von Meck, *Beloved Friend: the Story of Tchaikowsky and Nadejda von Meck* (London, 1937), p. 72.

[29] Gustave Reese, *Music in the Middle Ages* (New York, 1940), pp. 234–5. The song is recorded in *2,000 Years of Music* (Parlophone).

[30] G. F. Malipiero, *Claudio Monteverdi* (Milan, 1929), pp. 135–9.

[31] E. H. Fellowes, *William Byrd*, 2nd ed. (London, 1948), p. 10.

[32] Hans T. David and Arthur Mendel, *The Bach Reader*, 2nd ed. (New York, 1966), pp. 98–105.

[33] E. F. Rimbault, *The Old Cheque-Book, or Book of Remembrance, of the Chapel Royal* (London, 1872), pp. 60–1; *Calendar of State Papers, Domestic Series*, Sept. 1662 (p. 476), Sept. 2nd, Oct. 14th, 1662.

[34] *Calendar of State Papers, Domestic Series* (March) 1642 (p. 304).

[35] *The Diary of Samuel Pepys*, ed. Robert Latham and William Matthews, vol. vii (London, 1972), p. 414 (Dec. 19th, 1666).

[36] *Roger North on Music*, ed. John Wilson (London, 1959), pp. 355–6.

[37] C. S. Terry, *John Christian Bach*, 2nd ed. (London, 1967), p. 121.

[38] For details of Handel's finances see Erich H. Müller, *The Letters and Writings of George Frideric Handel* (London, 1935), pp. 63–74; Percy M. Young, *Handel* (London, 1947), pp. 228–32; W. C. Smith, *Concerning Handel* (London, 1948), pp. 9–64.

[39] The relevant letters are numbers 553–6, 567–9, 573–8, 580–3, 592–3 and 603 in Emily Anderson, *The Letters of Mozart and his Family*, 2nd ed. (London, 1966).

[40] Otto Erich Deutsch, *Schubert: a Documentary Biography* (London, 1946), pp. 932–4.

[41] Ibid., pp. 546–8.

[42] *Memoirs*, ed. David Cairns (London, 1969), p. 470.

[43] Summarized in Adam Carse, *The Orchestra in the XVIIIth Century* (Cambridge, 1940), pp. 18–27.

CHAPTER VII

THE MUSICIAN AND HIS ENVIRONMENT

WE have discussed at some length the economic background of musical history. We must now consider the musician's reaction to his environment. The term "environment" will obviously have two associated meanings. The first will refer to the particular circumstances in which the musician does his work—in other words, to the conditions of his employment and the extent to which he is affected by them. In the larger sense "environment" will also mean the domestic surroundings in which a musician lives and, more generally, the social structure of his country or period. It is clearly much easier to discuss the purely musical environment, in so far as it can be isolated, since the effect of environment in general is less obvious. A composer may pour into his music all the experiences of his daily life; but he may equally use his inspiration as a means of escape from circumstances which are wearisome or hostile to his art.

No one can study the music of the past without being impressed by the enormous number of works, both sacred and secular, which have been produced to order or to satisfy particular conditions. The realization of this fact is not always palatable to those who believe that music is simply the product of inspiration and like to imagine the great composers rolling in a fine frenzy whenever they set pen to paper. Inspiration, however, is an intangible quality which cannot be confined to any one channel; and centuries of experience have proved that the most prosaic stimulus can result in fine music. Two examples may be cited of eighteenth-century works which derive from particular

(Flocks and herds may graze contented
'Neath a watchful shepherd's care.
Kingdoms too on justice founded
Know the joys of peace unbounded,
And all happiness is there.)

The words of this aria are not calculated to inspire a composer. But the same might be said of many of the aria texts in Bach's church cantatas. As Schweitzer has pointed out, Bach

lived in the decadent epoch when music and poetry led each other astray, an epoch of excessive scribbling, of superficial art . . . an epoch which seemed fated to be impotent to create anything of durable value. . . . Of the innumerable cantatas that were written and admired at that time, his alone have survived their own day, and even these exhibit, both in their form and in their texts, traces of the dead world from which they have come.[4]

Bach's imagination was capable of taking fire from the most unpromising material. In this aria he forgets the main purpose of the text, which is to pay pompous tribute to a ruler, and devotes all his attention to the pastoral scene which is adduced as a parallel. This is in full accordance with eighteenth-century aesthetic theory, which believed that an aria should concern itself with one dominant "passion". There is, however, nothing conventional in Bach's application of this principle. The two recorders, inseparable from pastoral music, idealize the sound of sheep-bells, and the whole piece recalls the drowsy atmosphere of a summer's day. Everything here is basically the product of a particular time and a particular place; yet out of these raw materials, out of this mechanical necessity, Bach has created something universal. The aria which was designed for a specific purpose is today, in its original form and in numerous transcriptions, one of his most popular pieces.

For Bach necessity was nearly always the mother of invention. Circumstances dictated not only the character of his music but also the categories into which it falls. At Cöthen he occupied himself mainly with instrumental music since there was no opportunity of writing works for the Church. The Brandenburg concertos, as we have seen, were commissioned by a patron and would in all probability never have existed without that commission. At Leipzig he wrote some 300 church cantatas because these were required for the Lutheran services in St. Thomas's. His keyboard music was not written simply for entertainment but was often severely practical in intention. The manuscript title-page of the first part of *Das wohltemperirte Clavier* describes the preludes and fugues of that collection as composed "for the use and profit of the musical youth desirous of learning as well as for the pastime of those already skilled in this study". His two-part and three-part "Inventions" for keyboard were designed as a

straightforward introduction,[5] wherein the lovers of the key-board, and especially those desirous of learning, are shown a clear way not alone (1) to learn to play clearly in two voices, but also, after further progress, (2) to deal correctly and well with three *obbligato* parts; furthermore, at the same time not alone to have good *inventiones* [i.e. ideas], but to develop the same well, and above all to arrive at a singing style in playing and at the same time to acquire a strong foretaste of composition.

The purpose for which music was intended was always in the minds of eighteenth-century composers. Unlike the modern opera composer, who generally writes his opera first and then has to secure singers who can do justice to it, his eighteenth-century counterpart generally knew who the singers were going to be and wrote his music for them. For this reason we can never wholly recapture the spirit of Mozart's operas, because we have never heard the singers whom he had in mind. Like Bach and Handel he accepted the conventions of his time and yet had the clearest idea of what he wanted. In a letter about the composition of *Die Entführung* (see p. 35) he says that in Osmin's aria in Act I he has "allowed Fischer's beautiful deep notes to glow". Belmonte's aria "O wie ängstlich" was written "expressly to suit Adamberger's voice", and Constanze's "Trennung war mein banges Los" was "sacrificed . . . a little to the flexible throat of Mlle. Cavalieri".[6] This practical attitude was not new. We find it as early as 1770, when Mozart was only fourteen and had been commissioned to write *Mitridate Re di Ponto* for Milan. His father writes to his mother from Rome in June of that year:

> You ask whether Wolfgang has begun his opera? Why, he is not even thinking of it. You should ask us again when we have reached Milan on November 1st. So far we know nothing either about the cast or about the libretto.

And in November from Milan:

> Wolfgang has his hands full now, as the time is getting on and he has only composed one aria for the *primo uomo*, because the latter has not yet arrived and because Wolfgang refuses to do the work twice over and prefers to wait for his arrival so as to fit the costume to his figure.[7]

As for the conventions of opera, it is clear from the long series of letters about *Idomeneo*,[8] produced at Munich in 1780, that Mozart had his own ideas about dramatic propriety and was not prepared to accept any libretto without question.

Traditions varied from one country to another. In England the success of Handel's oratorios and their continued performance after his death made the oratorio a characteristically English form, accepted for at least 150 years as one of the most rewarding objects of a composer's attention. It is significant that many people were troubled by Sullivan's devotion to comic opera and felt that oratorio was his proper field. The English choral festivals helped to keep the oratorio alive and respected, and encouraged many composers of slender gifts to add to the repertory. If they had been living in Germany or Italy they would probably have written operas, which would have had no longer life than their oratorios. But opera in England offered few opportunities to native composers, and the oratorio remained the easiest way of making a reputation. These were the traditions in which Elgar grew up. Just as Verdi accepted the conventions of Italian opera, so Elgar accepted those of the oratorio; but in both cases a forceful personality and a growing maturity drove them farther and farther from what was merely conventional. *The Dream of Gerontius* would never have been written if oratorio had not been an accepted form of composition. But it displays gifts of imagination far beyond anything to be found in the work of Elgar's predecessors or contemporaries. Like Bach's *St. Matthew Passion* it is founded on tradition and yet remains an entirely personal work of art. Visitors to England were also affected by local traditions. Haydn's *Creation* was suggested by the popularity of *Messiah*, and the peculiar form of Weber's *Oberon* derives from the conventions of the English operatic stage in the early nineteenth century.

Beethoven was a rebel against convention, except in so far as it suited him to accept it. He wrote to please himself. Mozart may seem, at first sight, to have maintained that this was his own attitude to composition. He writes to his father in 1781:

I pay no attention whatever to *anybody's praise or blame*— I mean, until people have heard and seen the work *as a whole*. I simply follow *my own feelings*.[9]

But this does not imply rebellion against convention: it is simply the composer's expression of confidence in his own judgement. If Mozart had written only the works which he wanted to write we should have had a number of serious operas from the years of his maturity. We know that this was the type of opera which he liked to write; but circumstances compelled him to write *opera buffa*. Since those circumstances were responsible for the creation of *Figaro*, *Don Giovanni* and *Così fan tutte* we cannot very well complain: it is evident that Mozart had a genius for comedy. But it still remains true that there was a conflict between intention and achievement. With Beethoven it was different. After *Fidelio* he was continually looking for a libretto for another opera, but found none to satisfy him. When Rellstab asked him what type of poem he would like, he replied:

As to the type I am not so much concerned if only the subject-matter attracts me. Yet I must be able to take up my task with love and fervour. I could not compose operas like *Don Giovanni* and *Figaro*. I hold them both in aversion. I could not have chosen such subjects; they are too frivolous for me.[10]

It is true that he sometimes wrote music for special occasions. The overture *Weihe des Hauses*, written for a new adaptation of *Ruinen von Athen* in 1822, is an example. But Schindler tells us that the character of the piece was determined by the fact that Beethoven "had long cherished the plan to write an overture in the strict, expressly in the Handelian, style".[11] His most splendid ceremonial composition, the *Missa Solennis*, was meant for the installation of his friend the Archduke Rudolph as archbishop of Olmütz. But the work was not commissioned: the tribute was Beethoven's own idea, and the work was not, in fact, ready for the occasion for which it was intended. It is quite clear that much of his music was the product of a long period of gestation, which would have been quite unsuited to the conditions of eighteenth-century music-making. His ninth symphony, with choral finale, was completed in 1823; but sketches for it are found as early as 1798, and we know that even before that, when he was in his early twenties, he contemplated setting Schiller's ode "An die Freude".[12]

Schubert, like Beethoven, was independent, not so much from temperament as because he was not in a position to receive commissions. Much of his work was written for a friendly, middle-class circle, where domestic music-making was taken for granted. This social background was not without its influence on the types of music he wrote. In this society songs and piano duets were thoroughly at home, and Schubert was quite happy to write both. And these in turn had their effect on his other music. The influence of song on his instrumental works is obvious enough, quite apart from the fact that he used some of his own melodies as themes for variation; and the piano parts of his chamber music are often curiously like the *primo* part of a piano duet, with the strings providing the harmonic background. The work of the Romantic composers also was unmistakably determined by their environment, even though it is true that to some extent artists adopt the environment that suits their temperament. For Schumann, as for Schubert, music was very much a domestic art: he was not happy about his orchestration, and was hopelessly incompetent as a conductor. Wih piano music and songs he was thoroughly at home and quite ready to derive both from his own emotional experients. He tells us that

Carnaval came into existence incidentally, and is built for the most part on the notes A, S, C, H, the name of a small Bohemian town where I had a lady friend, but which, strange to say, are also the only musical letters in my name. The superscriptions I placed over them afterwards. For is not music itself always enough and sufficiently expressive? . . . The whole has no artistic value whatever; the manifold states of the soul alone seem to me of interest.[13]

The *Novelletten* were inspired by his love for Clara Wieck, who became his wife. He writes to her:

In the *Novelletten* you appear in every possible attitude and situation and all else that is irresistible in you . . . I assert that *Novelletten* could only be written by one who knows such eyes as yours and has touched such lips as yours. In short, better things might be made; similar ones, hardly.[14]

Compare this with the origin of Bach's *Musikalisches Opfer*, based on a theme supplied for extemporization by Frederick the Great (see p. 90). Schumann's songs were equally the expression of his romantic love. Exalted by the experience he cries (in 1840): "I should like to sing myself to death like a nightingale".[15]

The work of Liszt and Chopin makes a striking contrast. Both these composers wrote for fashionable audiences. This is not to belittle their achievement or their originality. It is merely a recognition of the fact that though, like Schumann, they were Romantics, their environment and their reaction to it were wholly different. It was the showman in Liszt that prompted him to write his operatic transcriptions and fantasias—a form of composition from which Schumann, one feels, would have instinctively recoiled. And yet these works, so far from being contemptible or of merely ephemeral value, are masterly examples of their kind. Saint-Saëns goes so far as to say that if Liszt

is dealing with a work of a high order, such as *Don Giovanni*, he not only illuminates the beauties of it but adds a commentary of his own that gives us a new insight into them and helps us to appreciate more fully their supreme perfection and their immortal modernity.[16]

This is clearly extravagant. We do not need the transcriptions of Liszt or anyone else in order to be able to appreciate *Don Giovanni*. On the other hand the recognition of the highly personal and strongly imaginative character of compositions of this kind, designed though they were to charm and astonish, is valuable and suggestive.

Wagner was less fortunate. The nature of his work was such that he had to make immense efforts to secure performances, until eventually he had won a sufficient number of supporters to make Bayreuth possible. We have a first-hand account of the frantic energy which he put into his playing of the second act of *Tannhäuser* when he was trying to persuade Léon Carvalho, director of the Théâtre-Lyrique, Paris, to perform it in 1859:

> He sang, he shouted, he threw himself about, he played the piano with his hands, his wrists, his elbows, he smashed the pedals, he ground the keys.[17]

Carvalho himself confirms the story:

> He howled, he threw himself about, he hit all kinds of wrong notes, and to crown it all he sang in German![18]

When eventually *Tannhäuser* was performed in Paris—not at the Théâtre-Lyrique but at the Opéra—it was a failure because Wagner had refused to conform to French convention and provide a ballet in the second act: the members of the aristocratic Jockey Club, who were in the habit of arriving late, were furious at being denied the opportunity of seeing their favourite dancers and provoked a violent demonstration.

Verdi's difficulties in Italy were of a different kind. As we have seen, he had no hesitation in accepting the operatic conventions in which he was brought up. He did not accept them idly, and he did not hesitate to modify them to suit himself.

When a singer asked him to write another aria for Gilda in
Rigoletto he replied:

"I have conceived *Rigoletto* without arias, without final tableaux,
just as an endless succession of duets because this form alone
satisfied me." If others say: "He should have done thus and thus",
I answer: "That may well be so, but what I have done is the best
I can do".[19]

At the same time there is nothing to show that the public was
aware of any revolution in style, and the music aroused no
protests. The protests came from the Austrian censor
(since the opera was produced at Venice, then part of the
Austrian Empire), and they were made several months
before the performance took place. The military governor
commented on "the revolting immorality and obscene
triviality" of the libretto (originally entitled *La Maledizione*)
and banned any performance of the opera. It was only with
great difficulty that he was persuaded to reconsider his
decision. Even then he asked for alterations—the duke must
not appear as a libertine, there must be no curses, Rigoletto
must not be a hunchback. Verdi refused to accept these
alterations on the ground that they completely changed the
character of the work. Eventually his persistence won the
day: the only change admitted was in the scene, which was
no longer to be the French court. The whole story illustrates
very vividly how strongly Italian composers were normally
bound by social conventions imposed on them by authority.

Such interference by the State is unusual at the present
day, except in Russia. Operatic conventions, however, are
not dead, in spite of the assaults of realism. If they were, the
public would reject many of the operas in the standard repertory as being ludicrously at variance with modern taste.
There is a commercial element in the production of operas
which has made many composers reluctant to abandon

lyricism, even if they wanted to. Menotti's success as an opera composer—notably in *The Consul*—has been due not simply to the emotional impact of a contemporary subject but also to the use of elements which are thoroughly familiar to the opera-going public. Professor Dent suggests a further influence in the case of Puccini:

His operas had to be up to date, with all the post-Wagnerian technique, but at the same time they had to be all divisible into sections that would each make a gramophone record.[20]

This is, no doubt, an attractive theory but it will not bear serious examination. At the time when *La Bohème* (1896) and *Tosca* (1900) were written the commercial possibilities of gramophone recording had hardly been realized. It is difficult to believe that Puccini foresaw these possibilities when writing his earlier operas, and there is no evidence that he was influenced by them in the composition of his later works.

Non-operatic forms of music in the twentieth century have been less affected by consideration for the public. This is particularly true of instrumental music. There has been a tendency on the part of some composers to write works which appeal only to a very limited circle, and which indeed are sometimes unintelligible to anyone outside the circle. The growth of small cliques has produced conditions which are in some way similar to those already noted in the sixteenth century—the provision of music for a small number of connoisseurs. The resemblances, however, are superficial. The connoisseurs of the sixteenth century were simply men whose education or wealth or both inclined them to pursue the art of music. They did not claim a peculiar enlightenment which enabled them to understand the work of a few composers who were not otherwise appreciated. It is true that a distinction was recognized between *musica comuna* and *musica riserbata* (or *musica reservata*): the first was music of a simple and direct character, suitable for public occasions and a large audience, the second implied a style akin to chamber music, in which the meaning of the words was subtly translated into music in a way which only educated people could understand. But the people who listened to *musica reservata* did not form independent cliques: they were not oases in a large world of cultivated music-lovers. They were themselves the world of music-lovers, and it was of necessity a narrow world. The situation today is very different. We find composers writing for small circles of people who are not superior in taste or breeding but who, for one reason or another, take pleasure in music which is alien to the majority of music-lovers. While there is no reason in general to doubt the sincerity of such admiration, the dangers are obvious enough, since there will always be vain and weak-minded people who will be tempted to ally themselves with a small minority, without ever understanding what they profess to admire.

Outside such limited circles one of the most potent influences on composers is the example of their predecessors. The great composers, as we have seen, begin by accepting the conditions in which they have been brought up. As they mature they develop a personal and individual style, without necessarily rejecting those conditions. Or alternatively a group of composers, influenced strongly by local or national traditions, may write in a style which has its roots in the temperament of a particular race or a particular community. But since in music there are no frontiers, these personal and local idioms have often been widely adopted by subsequent composers and often find their way into the commonplaces of popular music. The revival of Bach's music in the nineteenth century not only had a marked effect on many Romantic composers but also established a model of contrapuntal writing which is still a necessary foundation of a serious composer's technique. It is interesting equally to note how Wagner, a rebel against convention, became one of the most widely imitated of nineteenth-century composers: the influence of his harmonic idioms and his sonorous orchestration spread far beyond the confines of Germany. In the sphere of popular music we may note how readily the idioms of the Russian nationalists and of composers like Debussy and Delius have been absorbed into the stock-pot which provides the ingredients for film music, the tea-shop and the jazz band.

When we come to examine the environment of composers in a more general sense we naturally find a considerable diversity; and it may be doubted whether it is possible to find any common denominator which will explain the fecundity or the quality of musical invention. Material prosperity is certainly no criterion. Few people nowadays would be sentimental enough to claim that every artist ought to work in a garret. It is true that art may very often arise from adversity, but not from crippling adversity. Musicians, like everyone else, need money, and they cannot be expected to work properly unless they enjoy conditions comparable with those that would be considered indispensable in the case of a bank clerk or an engine-driver. Mendelssohn and Meyerbeer are sometimes cited as examples of composers who were too comfortable to become artists of the first rank. The argument, however, is specious, since neither of the two showed any inclination to take life easily: Mendelssohn killed himself by overwork, and Meyerbeer was excessively conscientious. Whatever shortcomings these two composers may have had, the fault lay in themselves and not in their upbringing. Provided a composer has enough to live on, there seems no reason why his music should reflect the material conditions of his everyday existence. There is nothing in the music of Byrd's *Gradualia* to suggest that the composer was constantly engaged in litigation.

Nor are domestic conditions necessarily either a spur or a

handicap. Marriage appears to be no criterion of artistic independence. Many eminent composers have been bachelors —among them Handel, Beethoven, Schubert, Chopin, Brahms, Sullivan, Wolf and Ravel. Many again have been married, some more than once: they include Lassus (who wrote a motet to the charming words "Sponsa, quid agis, mea lux?"), Palestrina, Monteverdi, Purcell, Bach, Haydn, Mozart, Schumann, Wagner, Berlioz and Debussy. It is quite impossible to draw any conclusions from these lists, and the task would be no easier if they were to be made exhaustive, instead of merely representative. Even if we examine these relationships closer and pry into the private lives of married men, we are no better off. Schumann was happily married to Clara, Wagner to Cosima. On the other hand Haydn's married life was thoroughly unhappy, Berlioz was separated from his first wife for thirteen years, and Debussy's first marriage ended in divorce. Mozart's marriage, though happy, might be regarded as unsuccessful, since his wife seemed unable to supply the business-like qualities which he lacked, though curiously enough she became extremely practical after his death, particularly in dealing with publishers. Yet none of these last four composers seems to have been adversely affected by his matrimonial experiences. What the effect of such experiences would have been on composers who managed to avoid them it is impossible to say, though it is not difficult to imagine that Schumann would have fallen a victim to mental instability much earlier if his union had ended in disaster.

In spite of the difficulties which any generalization presents there are none the less examples of personal relationships which had some effect on composition. Some of these were incidental, others were more profound. Though we cannot be absolutely certain, it is not extravagant to imagine that the death of Monteverdi's wife in 1607 prompted the intense emotion which found expression in the heroine's lament in *Arianna* in the following year. With some other composers the facts are not in dispute. Bach has outlined clearly the programme behind his keyboard Capriccio in B♭. It bears the sub-title "sopra la lontananza del suo fratello dilettissimo" (on the departure of his dear brother), and the several movements depict the emotions and the excitement proper to the occasion. Some of this is playful in intention— for example, the fugue on the posthorn tune; but there is no mistaking the sincere feeling expressed in the earlier movements. In Mozart's career nothing is more striking than the way in which his maturity as a composer corresponds with his maturity as a man, typified by his marriage to Constanze in 1782 (in spite of his father's opposition) and his decision to make an independent career for himself in Vienna. It is a strange, but not insignificant coincidence, that the heroine of *Die Entführung* (first performed in the same year) was also called Constanze. The subject of that opera is the attempt to deliver the lady and her maid from a Turkish harem. Mozart's marriage cannot strictly be called a "runaway match";[21] but at least it showed a healthy disregard of parental authority.

The connexion between Schumann's romantic passion for Clara Wieck and the composition of his songs has already been noted. The nature of such a connexion, however, needs to be carefully defined. Too little is known about inspiration for us to be able to assert that any personal relationship is directly responsible for a work of art. The idea of the *femme inspiratrice* is naturally popular with women and has often been accepted by sentimental biographers; but in fact all that we can say for certain in such a case is that passionate attachment to an individual may heighten the sensibility of a creative artist. In consequence he may be more ready to pour forth what might otherwise have been withheld; but whatever he creates is a part of him and of him only, and it was already implicit in his imagination before he received any stimulus from another. This is equally true of Wagner's

Tristan, which has sometimes been represented as the consequence of his passion for Mathilde Wesendonck. In fact the influence may very well be the other way round: a passionate urge to create may exaggerate the individual's susceptibility to personal attractions.

Scenery is also a powerful stimulus to composition. We find Mendelssohn in Scotland quoting in a letter the opening bars of what was to become the *Hebrides* overture, "to show how extraordinarily the place affected me". The scherzo of Elgar's second symphony is said to have been suggested by the flight of doves over Venice. But over and above these obvious influences there is the whole field of everyday experience, any detail of which, however casual and capricious it may seem, may set the springs in motion. In all these cases, as in personal relationships, it may be argued that there is already a predisposition to create: all that experience does is to stir the composer to action. We have an interesting parallel in the influence of folksong on the work of Vaughan Williams and some of his contemporaries in England. "Several of us," he has said, "found here in its simplest form the musical idiom which we unconsciously were cultivating in ourselves, it gave a point to our imagination." And again: "Here was something entirely new to us and yet not new. We felt that this was what we expected our national melody to be, we knew somehow . . . that this was just what we were looking for."[22]

Romantic artists were so conscious of the world around them that they often tended to exaggerate the importance of stimuli. Berlioz writes about the composition of his *Symphonie fantastique* in the wildest terms:

I have just been plunged once more into all the anguish of an interminable and inextinguishable passion, devoid of both motive and subject. She is still in London, and yet I seem to feel her near me; all my former feelings for her are aroused, and combine

E

to tear me to pieces; I hear my heart beat, and its pulsations
shake me as though they were the strokes of the piston-rod of a
steam-engine.

I was on the point of commencing my great symphony
(*Épisode de la vie d'un artiste*), wherein the development of my
passion is to be portrayed; I have it all in my head, but I cannot
write a line.[23]

The succeeding letters, in the course of which he outlines
the programme of the symphony much as we know it today,
are equally extravagant. It appears from them that his passion
for Harriet Smithson changed rapidly to contempt, and that
for this reason the finale of the symphony represents a witches'
sabbath in which the beloved "n'est plus qu'une courtisane
digne de figurer dans une telle orgie".[24] One would imagine
that love and hate had joined forces to produce a highly
programmatic work. In actual fact much of the *Symphonie
fantastique*, including the *idée fixe* which portrays the beloved,
is borrowed from earlier works by the composer. The music
may have suggested the programme, but the programme
cannot possibly be said to have created the music: the only
inspiration which Berlioz derived from his love and contempt
for Harriet was the urge to use scissors and paste on a large
scale.

One cannot imagine Mozart practising such self-
deception. We have it on the authority of his wife that he was
working at his string quartet in D minor (K.421) during the
night of 17th–18th June, 1783, when she was in labour for five
hours. But all that Mozart himself tells us is that the child
was eventually born at half past six in the morning, that he
reluctantly agreed to the engagement of a wet nurse, and that
the boy was christened Raimund Leopold, after Baron
Wetzlar and his grandfather.[25] Nothing is said about
composition—no doubt for the very good reason that it had
no connexion whatever with his domestic anxieties. There is,
in fact, no reason why a composer's music should express his

reaction to his environment: it may very well be in conflict with it. Mrs. Powell (the "Dorabella" of the *Enigma Variations*) has related how the composition of one of the most moving and spiritual passages in Elgar's oratorio *The Kingdom* was the occasion for an exhibition of outrageous rudeness to his guest.[26]

Political and social circumstances have often affected the practice of music. In seventeenth-century England, for example, the Civil War had the immediate effect of silencing church music and so encouraging the cultivation of secular forms. Roger North, in the reminiscences which he compiled in his old age, goes further and suggests that the war particularly favoured the practice of instrumental music, "for many chose rather to fidle at home, then [i.e. than] to goe out & be knockt on the head abroad".[27] On the Continent the Thirty Years War had quite a different effect. The conflict between Catholics and Protestants intensified the cultivation of Protestant church music and so created the soil in which eventually Bach's genius was to strike its roots. When we turn to the late eighteenth century we cannot help noticing how strongly Beethoven, the most original composer of his time, reacted to the French Revolution—a political upheaval whose effects spread far beyond the borders of France.

To a twentieth-century observer, aware of all the international bloodshed which has defiled European civilization since 1800, the liberalism of Beethoven and his contemporaries may seem a little naïve. We can appreciate the warmth of their belief in the brotherhood of man, but we cannot help contrasting it with the way in which subsequent history made it appear a mockery. Mercifully Beethoven was spared a vision of the future; to him this belief was no sentimental wishful thinking but an article of faith. The last props of feudalism were falling, and there seemed the promise of a world in which men might be free of the shackles of tyranny. All this is powerfully expressed in Schiller's ode to joy, which Beethoven set as the finale of the ninth symphony. But it appears equally in the last scene of *Fidelio* and in the music to *Egmont*, and frequently in music to which no specific programme is assigned: to anyone familiar with Beethoven's thought the last movement of the fifth symphony sings of the millenium as plainly as any setting of words. This faith in mankind was strong enough to withstand the cruellest disappointment. His pupil, Ferdinand Ries, tells us that Beethoven originally intended his third symphony as a tribute to Napoleon; but when he heard that Napoleon had proclaimed himself emperor he was furious and ripped off the title-page, on which the name "Bonaparte" had been inscribed.[28] The incident may appear trivial, but in its way it emphasizes the composer's ruthless sincerity more vividly than the positive affirmation of *Egmont* or the ninth symphony.

In so far as Beethoven shared these views with many of his enlightened contemporaries we may say that his music reflects the spirit of the age. The generalization, however, is a dangerous one, since it is never possible to define exactly the spirit of any age. How, for example, are we to characterize the ages notable for the music of Handel, Mozart, Elgar or Ravel? Every age shows strong contrasts, both of thought and of behaviour, and no artist can hope to offer a faithful reflection of it. In fact no genuine artist would try to do anything of the kind. Beethoven was not consciously attempting to provide a musical counterpart to the liberalism of his day: his music was an expression of himself, and is only "liberal" in the sense that these beliefs were an inseparable part of his character. Much of his music is entirely free from any suggestion of protest against an existing order, and this is true of most composers: their art, like the age in which they live, has many facets. It is sometimes said that Vaughan Williams's symphony in F minor is a picture of the turbulent world in which it came to birth; but it is also the work of the man who wrote its serene and sanguine successor in D major. There are times when an artist is powerfully affected by the world around him, and times when he is conscious only of the man within. While it is true that great music could only have assumed its form and character at the time at which it was written, it is equally true that it could only be the product of the individuals who created it.

[1] Otto Erich Deutsch, *Handel: a Documentary Biography* (London, 1955), pp. 573–4.

[2] Printed by F. Chrysander as Supplement No. 2 to his edition of Handel.

[3] See *Handel and his Orbit* (London, 1908), and "Handel, or Urio, Stradella and Erba" in *Music and Letters*, Oct. 1935, pp. 269–77.

[4] Albert Schweitzer, *J. S. Bach*, trans. Ernest Newman (London, 1911), vol. i, pp. 95–6.

[5] The original German is "auffrichtige Anleitung", which is translated by Ernest Newman (Albert Schweitzer, *J. S. Bach*, vol. i, p. 328) as "an honest guide", and by Arthur Mendel (*The Bach Reader*, p. 86) as "upright instruction". "Upright" is a little ambiguous. The adjective *aufrichtig* means "faithful, sincere, genuine". *Anleitung* is not strictly "instruction"; it means literally "introduction"—in this case an introduction to a method of study. The whole phrase implies a sincere intention to lay the foundations of part-playing and composition. The remainder of the above translation is from *The Bach Reader*, loc. cit., with the substitution of "keyboard" for "clavier".

[6] Emily Anderson, *The Letters of Mozart and his Family*, 2nd ed. (London, 1966), p. 769.

[7] Ibid., pp. 146, 171.

[8] Ibid., pp. 659–709.

[9] Ibid., p. 756.

[10] *Beethoven: Impressions of Contemporaries* (New York, 1927), p. 182.

[11] A. W. Thayer, *The Life of Ludwig van Beethoven*, ed. Elliot Forbes (Princeton, 1964), p. 807.

[12] Ibid., p. 121.

[13] Frederick Niecks, *Robert Schumann* (London, 1925), p. 176.

[14] Ibid., p. 201. The title *Novelletten* is an allusion to the singer Clara Novello, because she had the same Christian name.

[15] Ibid., p. 206.

[16] Quoted in Ernest Newman, *The Man Liszt* (London, 1934), pp. 213–14.

[17] Agénor de Gasperini, quoted in Ernest Newman, *The Life of Richard Wagner*, vol. ii (London, 1937), p. 547.

[18] Ibid., p. 548.

[19] F. Bonavia, *Verdi* (London, 1930), p. 60.

[20] Edward J. Dent, *Opera* (London, 1940), p. 112.

[21] Eric Blom, *Mozart* (London, 1935), p. 118.

[21] R. Vaughan Williams, *National Music* (London, 1934), pp. 75, 82.

[22] *Lettres intimes* (Paris, 1882), pp. 63–4, translated in W. J. Turner, *Berlioz, the Man and his Work* (London, 1934), p. 125.

[24] Ibid., p. 68 (Turner, op. cit., p. 128).

[25] Emily Anderson, *The Letters of Mozart and his Family*, 2nd ed. (London, 1966), pp. 851–2.

[26] Mrs. Richard Powell, *Edward Elgar : Memories of a Variation*, 2nd ed. (London, 1949), pp. 69–73.

[27] *Roger North on Music*, ed. John Wilson (London, 1959), p. 294.

[28] *Beethoven : Impressions of Contemporaries* (New York, 1927), p. 54.

CHAPTER VIII

THE INFLUENCE OF TASTE

QUITE apart from the impact of particular beliefs on individual composers music in general may be influenced by doctrine. This is true of all church music of the past, and of twentieth-century music written in accordance with a specific ideology. Such music is judged, and must always be judged, by the extent to which it serves the particular purpose for which it is designed. This principle is not affected by the fact, already mentioned, that opinions have differed widely from one age to another, and sometimes even in the same age, as to what is or is not appropriate to this purpose. At any one period there has generally been an officially accepted attitude to church music, to which composers have been required to conform: a good example is the desire of the English reformers in the sixteenth century for simplicity and clarity, which resulted in a radical change in the style of English church music. Outside the sphere of church music judgement is not normally bound by any adherence to doctrine. Conventions may become established, snobbery may dictate uniformity, but rebellion does not imply unorthodoxy and individuals are free to think for themselves. The proverb *de gustibus non disputandum* cannot be taken literally to mean that taste is not a subject for argument, since it has often been a matter for dispute. Its truth lies rather in the suggestion that such a dispute can arrive at no conclusive result, since there is no final court of appeal.

In the history of music taste is of paramount importance. It is significant that the French and Italian words for taste— *goût* and *gusto*—mean also "style"; and in the eighteenth

135

century both these words were in use in Germany as well as in the countries of their origin. The original title of Bach's Italian Concerto is "Concerto nach Italiaenischen Gusto", which may equally well be translated "concerto in the Italian style" or "concerto according to the Italian taste". Some ten years earlier François Couperin in France published a collection of chamber sonatas entitled *Les Goûts réunis* (The United Tastes), the intention of which was to recognize the merits of the Italian, as well as of the French, style. Couperin also used the word *goût* to refer to the style of performance. In his didactic work *L'Art de toucher le clavecin* (1716) he mentions that several harpsichord-players have done him the honour of consulting him "sur la manière et le goust de toucher mes pièces".[1]

It is important to remember that up to the end of the eighteenth century "taste" meant normally aristocratic taste. There was popular music, but there was no such thing as popular taste, since there was no public for artistic music as there is today. Church music was written to fulfil a liturgical function or to honour a patron or simply for the glory of God. Secular music was written for a limited circle. The English madrigal was never a popular form of art: it was written to be performed in aristocratic or wealthy households, either by professional musicians or by amateurs whose education made them competent to tackle the difficulties. Ability to sing or play was regarded as a fashionable accomplishment, not necessarily to be attempted for artistic reasons. A writer of Charles I's reign has a characteristic comment on the education of a farmer's daughter:

If her father thrive on his Farme, the poore neighbours put the mastership upon him, and if she learne to play on Virginalls, 'tis thought a Courtlike breeding.[2]

Even after the Restoration Pepys could remark with surprise that a certain Ben Wallington

did sing a most excellent bass, and yet a poor fellow, a working
goldsmith, that goes without gloves to his hands.[3]

Many years later, in a letter to the Master of University
College, Oxford (1700), he expresses a more generous
attitude, in a passage which deserves inclusion in any
anthology of tributes to the art of music. Music, he says, is

a science peculiarly productive of a pleasure that no state of life,
publick or private, secular or sacred; no difference of age or
season; no temper of mind or condition of health exempt from
present anguish; nor, lastly, distinction of quality, renders either
improper, untimely, or unentertaining.

But even then he adds:

Witness the universal gusto we see it followed with, wherever
to be found, by all whose leisure and purse can bear it.[4]

The essence of aristocratic taste was refinement. The
Italian madrigal of the sixteenth century was an attempt to
match fine poetry with fine music—an entertainment
designed for people of culture who would be capable of
appreciating both. It was also closely related to the humanism
which saw in classical studies the foundation of education and
which, transplanted to England, created the English public
school. The world of Theocritus and Virgil's *Eclogues* made
a particular appeal, no doubt because the complete unreality
of its pastoral conventions seemed to provide an escape from
the hard realities of everyday life. The great bulk of madrigal
verse is pastoral and amorous: it was the aim of composers to
match the pastoral vein in their music and to underline the
conceits of love which form so large a part of the subject-
matter. In the early seventeenth century these conventions
passed over naturally into the solo cantata, and they were
still alive in the early eighteenth century. They were also

inevitably adopted in the first essays at drama with music and so provided the foundation for the earliest operas. To a sternly realistic observer the whole thing is a sham, a world of artifice and make-believe created for the amusement of people fortunate enough, in Pepys's words, to have both "leisure and purse". Yet from the acceptance of these conventions grew a wealth of exquisitely mannered and subtly expressive music, which still has power to charm in the widely different social conditions of the present day.

Leisure and wealth made possible foreign travel. Connoisseurs were quick to appreciate the art of other countries and hence to acquire a taste for foreign music. When they returned to their native land they brought with them manuscripts and printed books which passed from hand to hand and helped to arouse a similar enthusiasm among those who were either unable or unwilling to go abroad. By modern standards the transport of any age before the invention of the railway and the steamship was primitive; but these material obstacles did nothing to weaken the zest for travel. From the sixteenth century to the end of the eighteenth Italian music had an extraordinary vogue in other countries, partly because of its refinement and partly, no doubt, because the Mediterranean temperament made a powerful appeal to the inhabitants of northern Europe. Madrigal, cantata, opera, oratorio, sonata and concerto all came to birth in Italy; and all of these, in greater or less degree, found a welcome beyond the Alps. Even where local conditions delayed the adoption of a particular form, as was the case in seventeenth-century England, the style was rapidly assimilated.

It is particularly interesting to see how composers of other countries surmounted the obstacle of a different language. Italian is rich in feminine endings, and these are naturally part of the staple material of Italian verse, as represented in madrigal texts and opera librettos. They also provide a large number of convenient rhymes. The English language is far less rich in this respect: many translators of Italian librettos have found themselves over and over again having recourse to present participles at the ends of lines, with the inevitable inversions of sentences which this procedure so often involves. The English madrigal composers required texts which would enable them to write an Italianate music: hence the authors of these texts, generally anonymous, were sometimes hard put to it to provide the feminine endings which were required. We meet absurdities like

> Sing we and chant it
> While love doth grant it

from Morley's *Balletts*, where the monosyllable "it" is virtually meaningless. This devotion to Italian rhythms persists throughout the seventeenth century and may be observed in the texts of Handel's English oratorios and cantatas. The author of *Acis and Galatea*, having embarked blithely on

> O ruddier than the cherry,

was forced to continue:

> O sweeter than the berry!
> O nymph, more bright
> Than moonshine night,
> Like kidlings, blithe and merry,

with even more artificial rhymes in the second verse. When, as not infrequently happened, the English poets were content with masculine endings, composers often seized on a feminine ending in the middle of a line and used it to provide a typically Italian cadence. Notice, in Purcell's well-known song "I attempt from love's sickness to fly in vain", how he extracts the word "fever" in the second line. Handel supplies many similar examples. So characteristic was the feminine ending that it affected also Italian instrumental music and, in fact, became a common cliché in an allegro movement. Composers of other nationalities who imitated the Italian style automatically copied the cliché. We hear it in the opening bars of Bach's Italian Concerto and in hundreds of other sonatas and concertos of the same period. What began as a purely local mannerism, conditioned by a particular language, became an international idiom.

The one country which stubbornly resisted the Italian style was France. One reason for this may be the difference of language. Unlike Italian, German and English, French has no tonic accent. This not only makes it possible for French composers to put any syllable in an accented position but has also resulted in a curiously fluid style of writing which has persisted down to the present day and has left its mark on instrumental music. The antithesis between such music and the clearly pointed Italian style is obvious. But there is another reason for the French refusal to surrender to the Italian invasion, and that is what can only be called, paradoxically, the "insularity" of Frenchmen, who are in general firmly convinced that their own traditions and conventions are superior to anything else in the world. So strong is this attitude that foreign composers like Lully and Cherubini who have become domiciled in France have written music which is as obstinately French as any work by a native of the country. It is true that there are examples in French music of the adoption of Italian mannerisms. But these occur only occasionally, and are generally deliberate imitations, such as Couperin's *L'Apothéose de Corelli* or the *airs italiens* introduced into eighteenth-century operas; and even then the foreign mantle hardly conceals the Frenchman underneath. It is equally true that the success of Pergolesi's *La serva padrona* in Paris in 1753 led to a violent campaign in favour of Italian comic opera (the *guerre des bouffons*, or the "comedians' war"). But although this gave a spur to the composition of French comic opera, it did not turn it into a mere copy of an Italian model: *opéra-comique* remained obstinately French in idiom and in presentation.

The insularity of the French did not prevent other countries from admiring their music. Though Italian music was in high favour in Restoration England there was also admiration for the French style of instrumental music. In particular the French overture—a stately, pompous introduction followed by a fugal allegro—was widely adopted in Europe, both as an introduction to operas or other large-scale works and as the prelude to a suite of dances. The enthusiasm of German rulers for French culture and their envious respect for the splendour of Versailles have already been mentioned (p. 95). We can see the reflection of this attitude in hundreds of instrumental works by German composers—for example, Georg Muffat's *Florilegium* (1695–98), Bach's orchestral overtures (or suites) and Telemann's *Musique de table*. Among the French mannerisms which had a far-reaching effect was the practice of writing the middle section of a minuet for three wind instruments (as Bach does in the first Brandenburg concerto): the name "trio" for such a section survived long after this practice became obsolete, and was still in use by Romantic composers in the nineteenth century.

In the baroque period—roughly the seventeenth and early eighteenth centuries—there was an increasing tendency for musical forms and musical expression to become stereotyped. Recitative, which began as a highly expressive type of musical declamation, rapidly developed into a series of conventional formulas, which most eighteenth-century composers could have written in their sleep. Only in the accompanied recitative—that is to say, the recitative with orchestral accompaniment as opposed to the *recitativo secco* (dry recitative) with keyboard—did composers fully exercise their imagination: here the opportunity was taken to express a wide range of emotions, often by means of strongly contrasted dynamics and extravagant modulation. Arias in opera acquired familiar lineaments which appear over and over again in the work of widely different composers. German writers of the early eighteenth century evolved a precise doctrine of musical expression. One has only to turn at random the pages of Handel's operas or oratorios to see how consistently the emotions of defiant rage, baffled fury, tender sentiment and pastoral tranquillity are expressed. Instrumental obbligatos were equally standardized—the trumpet for heroic arias, the horn for hunting scenes, the recorder or flute for any suggestion of bird-song.

The strong pressure of aristocratic taste contributed towards the changes of instrumental style which took place in the course of the eighteenth century. Contrapuntal elaboration was looked on with disfavour because it was difficult to follow, canons were despised. The patrons of music were not necessarily educated music-lovers: they preferred music which was simple and direct in its appeal but at the same time elegant and refined in its expression. Composers of eighteenth-century symphonies concentrated more and more on writing works in which expressive or vivacious melodies were clearly outlined above a simple accompaniment. Wind instruments were found useful for sustaining or filling in the harmony, and the keyboard continuo of the early eighteenth century gradually fell into disuse. Mozart, who learned from his study of Bach the value of expressive counterpoint, was by no means typical of his period; and there must have been many listeners who found his music difficult to follow. The doctrine of simplicity was preached in its most extravagant form by Rousseau, who wanted music to return to nature; but unfortunately he lacked the necessary qualifications to give a convincing demonstration of what he meant.

Throughout the eighteenth century the extraordinary popularity of opera supplies a solid background to the fluctuations of musical taste. Not only was the opera overture the begetter of the classical symphony, but often the accents of the operatic aria or the operatic ensemble are to be heard in purely instrumental compositions. The slow movements of sonatas and symphonies constantly suggest a singer with accompaniment. In Mozart, who was so passionately devoted to opera, the associations with the stage are constantly apparent. The concluding Presto of the finale of the G major piano concerto (K.453), is exactly like one of those dramatic ensembles in which rival groups face each other across the stage, while plot and counterplot are translated into symphonic terms. Quite apart from such direct similarities many of the conventions of dramatic music—the sudden sforzandos, the restless pizzicato basses, the diminished sevenths— were appropriated by composers of instrumental music, so that the symphony itself became in many ways a dramatic form.

The breakdown of feudalism, to which we have already referred, changed the whole character of music in the nineteenth century. Taste was no longer the prerogative of the leisured classes. Music made its appeal to a much wider public and penetrated into the homes of ordinary people. Nineteenth-century music is rich in examples of what might be called domestic music—the song without words, the piano duet, the romance. Works of this kind did not demand the virtuosity expected on the public platform. They were accessible to modest amateurs, and in many cases were composed for them. Composers discovered that there was a market for their wares, and were not slow to profit by the discovery. It was, however, some time before public taste became discriminating. A present-day audience would be insulted at the suggestion that it was incapable of listening to a complete symphony. But in the early years of the nineteenth century it was quite a common practice to relieve the strain on listeners by separating one movement from another. And if we may trust contemporary accounts the performances were often of a kind that not even the most uncritical audience of today would tolerate. It is significant that one of Beethoven's most popular pieces was *Wellington's Victory, or the Battle of Vittoria,* a pretentious and vulgar piece originally written for a mechanical instrument invented by Mälzel, who was also the creator of the metronome.

In Italy public taste was not a nineteenth-century development, since opera had appealed to more than an aristocratic circle ever since the first opera-house was opened in Venice in 1637. Burney, who visited Italy to collect materials for his history of music, has left us a vivid picture of the conditions under which opera was performed in the eighteenth century. He writes that the San Carlo theatre at Naples

surpasses all that poetry or romance have painted: yet with all this, it must be owned that the magnitude of the building, and noise of the audience are such, that neither the voices or instruments can be heard distinctly.[5]

The popularity of opera as a spectacle continued to dominate Italian music throughout the nineteenth century. The Italian critic Gian Andrea Mazzucato, writing of Milan in the 1860's, declares that

music and *opera* were synonymous words. . . . Even as late as 1876, the only copy of Beethoven's symphonies to be had at the Library of the Conservatorio was a cheap edition printed at Mendrisio, and so full of mistakes as to be in some parts unintelligible.[6]

It is hardly surprising that opera composers in Italy wrote

deliberately for a public which was nurtured on tradition. Where everything was subordinated to the singer there was little opportunity or inducement to aim at any higher scale of values. It was Verdi who rescued Italian opera from this standardized vulgarity; but it is only in comparatively recent years that the classics of instrumental music have come to be accepted in Italy as they have long been in other countries.

Public performance did not necessarily raise the standard of public taste. On the contrary public taste had a powerful influence on performers. In particular it encouraged the display of virtuosity. Solo performers had been highly esteemed from the beginning of the seventeenth century, and much of the instrumental music of this period, often extravagant in its demands, is a witness to the willingness of composers to serve the interests of virtuosos. In the opera house solo singers for long reigned supreme—and would do still, if it were not for the adulation now lavished equally on conductors. But the social changes which took place in the nineteenth century gave the solo performer, outside the theatre, the opportunity to appeal to a much wider public. Pianists delighted in astonishing their audiences by the brilliance of their fantasias and variations. Mendelssohn's *Variations sérieuses* were written as a protest against the superficiality of much of the piano music of the time. Paganini's feats on the violin seemed so miraculous that he was credited with supernatural powers. Even fine musicians like Liszt were not above yielding to the popular craze for sensation. Mendelssohn criticizes severely a recital by Liszt which he heard in Berlin in 1842:

He performed works by Beethoven, Bach, Handel and Weber in such a pitiably imperfect style, so uncleanly, so ignorantly, that I could have listened to many a middling pianist with more pleasure.

He goes on to detail some of the misdemeanours: omissions

F

of several bars, alteration of the harmony, misplaced dynamics.[7] These faults were not the product of carelessness but of a vainglorious desire to win applause at all costs.

The public is not so ignorant today. Solo performers are still idolized, but no audience would tolerate the deliberate perversion of familiar classics. The very word "classics" is significant of the growth of an educated public taste. Until the end of the eighteenth century secular performances were mainly of contemporary music. It was not only the musicians but the musical public in the nineteenth century who came to revere the works of dead composers, and to ensure their survival by a recurrent demand for performances. Among these music-lovers were many men of distinction in the other arts and learned professions; and since many musicians of the time had literary gifts and were themselves cultured men there grew up a new community of the arts, a new acceptance of the belief that music, no less than painting and literature, deserved the interest of educated men. The classics of music, by dint of repetition, came to be as solidly established as the classics of literature. The field was limited, but there were always ardent spirits who were anxious to extend it back in time. To their efforts we owe the revival of much splendid music of the past. While it may still be true that for the ordinary music-lover the classics of music include little before the time of Bach and Handel, there is none the less a respectable amount of earlier music which is familiar to anyone who takes the art seriously. Even medieval music, once regarded as impossibly remote, has come to life through broadcasting and gramophone records and has delighted listeners in a way which earlier historians would have thought quite impossible. All this has not been without its effect on composers, many of whom have grown up with a knowledge of plainsong and sixteenth-century polyphony, and have drawn energy from their experience without necessarily having recourse to deliberate imitation.

The new association between music and the other arts which developed in the Romantic age was largely responsible for the appearance of impressionism in music, which drew its inspiration from the French impressionist painters and the symbolists in poetry. The close association which had existed between Liszt and Chopin and the painters and poets of their day had its counterpart at the end of the century in Mallarmé's circle in Paris, where creative artists of every kind met on equal terms and pursued a common ideal. The reason why Debussy, leader of the musical impressionists, was never intimate with men like Verlaine and Renoir was not a lack of sympathy but a constitutional incapacity for close friendship with anyone—except perhaps Pierre Louÿs. Another characteristic of the times was the cult of exotic music, evidences of which are to be found frequently in the work of Debussy and Ravel. We may attribute this either to boredom with purely European idioms or possibly to the public interest aroused in anthropological research, part of which was concerned with the music of Oriental and primitive peoples. So strong was this influence, which even now is not dead, that it penetrated into the stronghold of Italian opera—most notably in Puccini's last opera *Turandot* (1926).

The most recent example of the effect of public taste on musical composition is to be found in the very con- siderable number of works written since the 1914–18 war in which jazz idioms are employed. This adoption of popular music into serious composition is rather different from the attitude to popular music taken in the sixteenth and seven- teenth centuries, when the tendency was to present a sophis- ticated and often completely transformed version of popular songs and dances. In the twentieth century the acceptance of vulgar clichés has been much more wholehearted. Works like Lambert's *Rio Grande* (1929) and Křenek's opera *Jonny spielt auf* (1927) make no bones about accepting the language of the dance hall and exploiting it for another purpose. By a strange irony jazz itself has acknowledged the influence of modern composers and made their idioms acceptable to ears which would never tolerate them in their proper setting. In a sense jazz may be said to be the one international idiom of our time, and its effect on the public has been quite different from the employment of purely national idioms which has made composers like Dvořák and Vaughan Williams, though respected abroad, most honoured in their own countries.

[1] *Oeuvres complètes* (Paris, 1933), vol. i, p. 25.
[2] Wye Saltonstall, *Picturae Loquentes*, 2nd ed. (London, 1635), No. 24.
[3] *Diary*, 15th Sept., 1667.
[4] *Private Correspondence and Miscellaneous Papers of Samuel Pepys, 1679–1703*, ed. J. R. Tanner (London, 1926), vol. ii, p. 109.
[5] *The Present State of Music in France and Italy* (London, 1771), p. 339.
[6] Quoted in Gerald Abraham, *A Hundred Years of Music*, 3rd ed. (London, 1964), p. 135.
[7] Ernest Newman, *The Man Liszt* (London, 1934), p. 10.

CHAPTER IX

THE STUDY OF MUSICAL HISTORY

THE preceding chapters have served to outline the subject and to suggest some of its implications. We have now to consider the purely practical question of how to study it. An indispensable foundation is the ability to read music—and not merely to read it but to hear it mentally. But this basic requirement is not all. Over and above a technical equipment which may be taken for granted the student needs imagination. This is true of the study of any art, but it is particularly true of music. The student of painting or architecture can learn a great deal by keeping his eyes open in a picture gallery or a cathedral. The material which he is studying is there before him and does not require to be recreated. There is no strictly comparable experience in music, partly because sound is fleeting and does not wait to be analysed and partly because music when performed reaches us only through the medium of an interpreter. We must also remember that only a small fraction of the music we shall want to study is likely to reach our ears—either in the concert hall or through radio or gramophone. It is true that broadcasting and recording have to some extent revolutionized the study of musical history, since the humblest beginner can now actually hear works which were previously known to professional historians only through the printed page. But it is obvious that we cannot be content merely to know what others have chosen to perform, quite apart from the fact that the authenticity of some of the performances may be open to serious question. We must ourselves scan the printed page, and in doing so continually make the effort to recreate the music in our own minds.

It must be admitted that historians have not always been helpful in meeting the student half-way. Many readers in the past must have been repelled by the mere appearance of the first volume of the *Oxford History of Music*—the musical examples with their rows of semibreves and minims, and the many pages devoted to the exposition of medieval theory. No wonder that medieval music was thought to be, if not dead, at least a purely primitive art, which had nothing to say to the music-lover of the present day. The error lay partly in the notation used for the examples, which suggested an art remote from any music which we know, and partly in the false emphasis laid on theoretical writings. Undoubtedly the study of theory is an essential part of the historian's task; but he will mislead both himself and his readers if he fails to realize that theory depends always on practice. Tunes are not constructed out of scales. The scales are a rationalization of the tunes, which existed long before scales were ever thought of. Medieval theory, like any other, is a codification of practice and hence, as we have seen already (p. 38), is generally out of date. Furthermore, since it is "monkish" it takes little account of music outside the Church and hence gives us not only an incomplete but a one-sided picture of the medieval scene.

Theory may help us to understand the music, but the music is what matters. As we study it we have an obligation to try to hear it as it was originally performed—or even better, if we have the necessary resources available, to perform it ourselves. We cannot be content merely to observe its structure or to recognize its idioms: we need also to rediscover its gaiety, earnestness, solemnity, devotion, or whatever other characteristics it may have. The farther the music from our own time the more difficult it becomes to discern the spirit behind the formal outline; and consequently, the farther back we go in musical history the greater is the need for exercising our imagination. This attitude must equally be maintained when we are dealing with a whole series of works of different periods and tracing the development of a form or a style. It is quite possible to study the history of polyphony as the development of technical procedures; but such a study is utterly meaningless unless we see it also as the growth of an art of expression. The fascination of contrapuntal writing lies not so much in the combination of different melodic lines as in the combination of contrasted rhythms. The ear is quite incapable of following a number of simultaneous melodies, but it is perfectly able to appreciate varieties of rhythm; and such variety naturally serves to heighten the interest of points of imitation. This is merely one example of the way in which the actual sound of music may be substantially different from what the eye observes.

The student of musical history must start always with the assumption that music, whatever its period may be, is alive. Music may be good or bad; but it cannot, once created, be dead, except in the sense that human beings may be described as dead souls if they lack any spark of imagination. Music of the past is not "quaint" or "old-world" because it is ancient. It demands our intelligent respect, and when we perform it we must see that the result is fresh and vivid. The obstacles to an authentic interpretation have been mentioned already in Chapter II. Some of them can be surmounted by intelligent study: others remain a problem. But however much the letter may elude us, we have no excuse for ignoring the spirit. If we are not constantly aware of music as a living art we might just as well abandon the study of it and turn our attention to the history of shipbuilding or sanitary engineering. We need the same approach to more recent music, whose very familiarity may tend to blind us to its intrinsic qualities. Nothing is gained by yielding conventional respect to Beethoven, merely because we have been told that he is one of the world's great masters or because tradition asserts that he is above criticism. We need to form our own judgements about him, to find our own reasons for admiration, and to hear his music, if possible, as his contemporaries did. Diminished sevenths are now the outworn small change of musical composition; but to Beethoven and his contemporaries they were charged with dramatic intensity, and unless we allow them to make this impression on us we miss much that is vital and significant. A proper conception of musical history involves "historical" listening—listening, that is to say, with the ears of another age and with all subsequent music banished from the mind. This direct apprehension of music is the basis of personal knowledge, just as a study of literary history involves knowing the authors as familiar friends.

As acquaintance with the work of individual composers improves, it becomes possible to correlate one's knowledge— to compare, for example, Purcell with Handel, or Mozart with Beethoven—and to work out a history of the principal episodes in the history of various forms. The results will of necessity be sketchy, since they will be to some extent based on a knowledge of isolated works; but in so far as they are based on personal acquaintance with the music, they will provide a more reliable outline than any popular summary designed for examination candidates. The picture will be completed for us by the historians, partly by emphasizing details whose significance had escaped our notice and partly by filling up the gaps in our knowledge and by drawing our attention to the lesser composers. We need to know something about the lesser composers, since they help us to appreciate more vividly the musical environment of the great men and the measure of their achievement. The hardest thing of all is to compare works of the same period or in similar styles— to be able to say precisely what are the differences between

Palestrina and Byrd, or between Bach and Handel. If we can do this, we have progressed beyond the mere accumulation of material towards a critical knowledge of styles and of individual idioms. And the more we can see the great composers in the round, the less likely we are to accept easy generalizations about their work. It should be impossible for anyone who has studied the history of music thoroughly to believe that Haydn's music was always gay or that Rossini was never serious.

However well we may know the work of the lesser men, it is inevitably the great composers whose achievement defines for us most sharply the periods in which they lived. The dangers and difficulties of periodization have been discussed in Chapter III. At the same time there is no harm in associating a period with a particular name, or with one or two names, provided we remember that the death of a great man does not close a period, and that any periods which we establish must inevitably overlap. A mere glance at the dates will be sufficient to establish the chronological relationship of Haydn, Mozart, Beethoven and Schubert and to avoid any idea that they come "after" each other as if they were segregated in watertight compartments. When Mozart died in 1791, Beethoven was nearly twenty-one and Haydn had more than seventeen years still to live. When Haydn died in 1809, Schubert was twelve and on the point of writing his first essays in composition. The only gap in years is between the death of Mozart and the birth of Schubert, and that is covered by Beethoven, who met them both. Dates in themselves are meaningless, but once they are related to each other they afford a useful method of correlating information and serve as a check on hasty generalization.

To the experienced student the mere mention of a date should stir up a whole host of associations, just as an address or a telephone number will bring to mind the characteristics and the activities of the people to whom they belong. Nor need these associations be confined to music. If we remember, for instance, that Purcell, Dryden, Wren and Newton were contemporaries (though not exact contemporaries) we have already some notion of the society for which Purcell's music was written. And when we come to the nineteenth century the relationship already mentioned between poets, painters and musicians makes it even more necessary to have a chronological framework into which they can be fitted.

Chronological study of this kind, embracing all aspects of a period, needs to be supplemented by a study of particular forms, of the resources available to composers, of the conditions for which they wrote, and of specialized subjects such as national music. Study of this kind is valuable since it provides a sort of cross-section of musical history and prevents one from losing important threads in the desire to achieve a complete survey. These various subjects are themselves inter-related, since the development of a form will be affected by the resources available and by social conditions, and will also be affected in different countries by differences of language and temperament.

We may take the concerto as a simple example of a form whose development can be studied through several centuries. The word itself is Italian. As early as the sixteenth century its etymology was disputed.[1] Was it from the Latin *concertare*, "to strive together" or the Latin *conserere* (past participle *consertus*), "to combine together"? In the Tuscan dialect the word was spelt and pronounced *conserto*, which might very well point to the second derivation. But quite apart from this possibility the types of music originally described as *concerti* do not in any way suggest strife or competition. The *Concerti ecclesiastici* of Viadana (1602) are simply compositions for one, two, three or four voices and *basso continuo*. The use of the term *concerto* to indicate works for voices with or without instruments was quite common at this time. Monteverdi described his seventh book of madrigals (1619) as *Concerto de madrigali*, and Giovanni Battista Doni, in his *Trattato della musica scenica* (written about 1635), speaks of the madrigal version of Monteverdi's *lamento d'Arianna* as a "concerto for several voices". Even a hundred years later we find Bach using the term *concerto* for the church cantata.

However, in the course of the seventeenth century the word came to be restricted more and more to purely instrumental music, and mainly to orchestral music. Thus a distinction developed between the sonata, in which there was normally one instrument to a part, and the concerto for a substantial ensemble. The distinction was made clearer by attaching to *concerto* the adjective *grosso* (large). A further development resulted from the seventeenth-century passion for instrumental virtuosity. Passages for solo instruments were written as a contrast to the main body of strings. Corelli's Op. 6 (1712) is entitled *Concerti grossi con duoi Violini, e Violoncello di Concertino obligati, e duoi altri Violini, Viola e Basso di Concerto Grosso ad arbitrio che si potranno radoppiare.* Here the term *concerto grosso* is used in two senses, first as a description of the composition as a whole, and secondly to denote the orchestra as opposed to the soloists (who also form part of it). Even here, as the concluding words show, the accompanying orchestra may consist of only one player to a part, though provision is made for doubling (*che si potranno radoppiare*). The group of soloists most frequently used consisted of two violins and cello, but many other groups were also used, and Vivaldi's concertos, in particular, make provision for a very wide variety of solo instruments.

It was natural that the emphasis on individual virtuosity should lead also to the practice of contrasting a single player with the orchestra. This development dates from the beginning of the eighteenth century. Here too Vivaldi supplies numerous examples. The model for such works was not only the instrumental style of the sonata and *concerto grosso*, but also the operatic aria with its alternation between orchestral ritornello and solo voice: in particular, the suave and expressive style of the slow aria had a marked influence on instrumental composers. The instruments used for the solo concerto were members of the orchestra, temporarily placed in a position of special responsibility. The harpsichord was regarded as a continuo instrument, used solely for filling up the harmony, and it was some time before anyone thought of writing a concerto for a keyboard instrument. It is significant that six of Bach's seven harpsichord concertos are adaptations of violin concertos and bear unmistakable signs of their origin. Handel's organ concertos owe their origin to the fact that he was in the habit of performing as a soloist in the intervals of his oratorios. By the middle of the eighteenth century the keyboard concerto was accepted as a form worth cultivating in its own right. Bach's second son, Carl Philipp Emanuel, wrote as many as fifty. But it was above all Mozart who created the model for all piano concertos by combining a subtle contrast between soloist and orchestra with a masterly handling of symphonic form.

Nineteenth-century composers of concertos tended to emphasize more than Mozart had done the superior execution of the soloist, and the increasing demands of virtuosity led to the writing of works in which the brilliance of the solo part was not always matched by the quality of the invention. It is reasonable here to see the consequence of the growth of a wider public for music. It is also the consequence of changes in the manufacture of pianos. The modern piano is a much more powerful instrument than Mozart's, as well as having quite a different tone. Hence the tendency in many piano concertos to pit the solo instrument against the full orchestra: the issue of the battle is never in doubt, since the orchestra can make more noise, but the struggle for mastery appeals to the naïve listener and is responsible for the

considerable vogue which such works still enjoy. It is
noticeable that concertos for other instruments have in
general been fewer in number since the beginning of the
nineteenth century. Beethoven, Brahms, Dvořák, Elgar,
Sibelius, Walton and Bartók have each written only one
violin concerto. But whatever the instrument employed and
however different the idiom may be, the basic principles of
writing a concerto have remained constant since Mozart's
time: a concerto, in fact, involves both contrast and co-
operation between soloist and orchestra. At the same time
some modern composers have revived the old idea of a
concerto for orchestra, without assigning a solo part to any
one instrument; examples are Bartók's Concerto for orchestra
and Hindemith's *Philharmonisches Konzert*, in which various
members of the orchestra are given an opportunity to
display virtuosity. Thus the wheel has come full circle, and
the *concerto grosso* lives again in another form.

This brief sketch, necessarily incomplete, will give some
idea of the way in which the development of a single form
can be studied through several successive periods. In all
such study one must bear in mind the relation of the particular form not only to other forms but also to the social
conditions in which it flourished. Thus the concerto cannot
be studied in isolation from opera and the symphony, and
equally one must take into account the differences in the
composition of the audiences for whom it was originally
intended. Whatever the subject may be that is studied in
this way it is essential for the student to ask himself not
merely "what?" but "why?"

It is fatally easy in all historical study to be content with
the facts and not to bother about the causes. In a good many
cases the professional historians will pose the problems
themselves; but any intelligent student is bound to discover
others for himself. He may be able to answer them without
much difficulty; others may resist immediate explanation

but may start a train of thought which will lead to original research. Such questions may not be concerned with specific points: they may be of the most general kind—for instance, what, if anything, is there in common between English composers? But whatever form they may take. in the effort to answer them the student will learn far more than he ever will by merely soaking up someone else's opinions from a book. Needless to say, the wider our education the better we shall be able to answer these questions. The more we know about the history of the world in general and the arts in particular, the more we are likely to see significance in details which at first sight seemed of little importance. The best equipped student of music is one who has also learned to educate himself.

In reading about the history of music it is always a sound principle to proceed from the general to the particular. No one should be too proud to read a work like Alfred Einstein's *Short History of Music*, the work of one who was deeply versed in the *minutiae* of musical scholarship but was at the same time able to take a balanced view of the whole field. This book has the merit of being very short: it is, of necessity, a bird's-eye view. But it is immensely stimulating to the reader, and often it makes clear in a few sentences matters to which other authors have devoted many pages. In reading a book of this kind we are bound to light on some facts which are familiar. Here is an excellent opportunity to test the author's opinions and to form our own judgement about his reliability as a guide. With his help we shall be able to make a preliminary attempt at deciding what are the really decisive things in the history of music and what are the outstanding achievements of each century. Once this basic survey is firmly fixed in the mind we can go on to read more detailed works, remembering always that scholarship does not stand still and that a book may be in some respects out of date as soon as it is published. Articles in musical periodicals will supply additional information, sometimes correcting what was formerly taken for granted, sometimes supplementing and amplifying the sources of our knowledge. Biographies and books on particular forms will also help to make the outlines clearer to our minds. And all the time the music must be our constant stand-by, the touchstone by which we test the views expressed by the historians and the evidence to which they constantly appeal. A clear mind is as necessary here as anywhere else in the field of knowledge. It is very easy to bandy about words like "polyphony", "classical", "romantic" and so on. What we need to do is to decide in our own minds what these terms mean, and to arrive at a point in our studies when the names of composers, of periods and of forms bring with them a whole world of associations. Only when we have reached that stage shall we begin to have a grasp of the subject; and only then shall we fully realize how vast is the territory still waiting to be explored.

[1] Hercole Bottrigari, *Il desiderio, overo de' concerti di varii strumenti musicali*, 2nd ed. (Bologna, 1599), p. 9; facsimile ed. by Kathi Meyer (Berlin, 1924). See also A. Einstein, *The Italian Madrigal* (Princeton, 1949), vol. ii, p. 821.

SOME RECOMMENDED BOOKS

(For reasons of space this list is confined to books in English)

General

W. D. Allen: *Philosophies of Music History* (New York, 1939).
A survey of histories of music from the earliest times, together with a critical examination of the methods and function of historians. The bibliography consists of a chronological list of 317 works.

W. Apel: *Harvard Dictionary of Music*, 2nd ed. (Cambridge, Mass., 1970).
A non-biographical dictionary, with abundant references to original sources and to modern works and articles in periodicals. The entry "Editions, Historical" is a convenient reference list of the contents of the more important series of editions of old music (excluding complete works of particular composers).

A. T. Davison and W. Apel: *Historical Anthology of Music*, 2 vols. (Cambridge, Mass., 1946–50).
A collection of 310 musical examples, many of which are complete pieces. The first volume deals with oriental, medieval and Renaissance music, the second is devoted to the seventeenth and eighteenth centuries. There are translations of the foreign texts, notes on the pieces and references to gramophone recordings.

A. Einstein: *A Short History of Music*, 5th ed. (London, 1948).
A compact but comprehensive summary, which includes an appendix of music examples. An illustrated edition, with more than 220 pictures but without the music examples, was published in 1953.

D. J. Grout: *A History of Western Music* (New York, 1960).
More substantial than Einstein's history and more concise
than Lang's. There are numerous illustrations and music
examples.

G. Kinsky: *A History of Music in Pictures* (London, 1930).
Over 350 pages of illustrations, including portraits of
musicians, representations of musical performance in painting
and sculpture, pages from manuscripts and printed works,
photographs of instruments, etc.

P. H. Lang: *Music in Western Civilization* (New York, 1941).
A substantial history of over 1,100 pages which constantly
relates music to the social and political conditions of its times
and to philosophy, literature and the other arts. There are a
number of illustrations but no music examples.

C. Parrish and J. F. Ohl: *Masterpieces of Music before 1750* (New
York, 1951).
An annotated anthology of fifty complete pieces or complete
excerpts from larger works.

C. Parrish: *A Treasury of Early Music* (London, 1959).
A companion volume to the above.

M. Pincherle: *An Illustrated History of Music* (London, 1960).
A superbly illustrated volume with an excellent historical
summary.

W. Wiora: *The Four Ages of Music* (New York, 1965).
An original survey of the changes in musical culture from
prehistoric times to the present day.

Periods
G. Abraham: *A Hundred Years of Music,* 3rd ed. (London 1964).
A study of the style and forms of Romantic and modern music,
together with chapters on musical conditions.

W. W. Austin: *Music in the 20th Century* (New York, 1966).
Discusses both the older and the more recent composers active
in the present century.

M. F. Bukofzer: *Music in the Baroque Era* (New York, 1947).
Covers the period from 1600 to the death of Handel. There are
several illustrations, over 100 short music examples, a list of
sources, and an index of books on music published during this
period.

H. C. Colles: *Symphony and Drama, 1850-1900* (London, 1934).
Originally Vol. VII of the *Oxford History of Music*. Special
attention is given to the music of Brahms and Wolf and to
Wagner's later operas. There is also a chapter on music in
England.

A. Einstein: *Music in the Romantic Era* (New York, 1947).
The author's aim is "to show how the Romantic movement was
manifested in music and how music affected the Romantic
movement". There are several portraits of composers, but
no music examples and no bibliography.

H. Gleason: *Examples of Music before 1400* (New York, 1942).
A collection of 101 pieces, transposed where necessary for
the benefit of performers but not otherwise re-edited.

New Oxford History of Music, vol. i: *Ancient and Oriental
Music,* ed. E. J. Wellesz (London, 1957).
This volume, as its title implies, deals with the music of
Greece and Rome, so far as it is known, and also embraces
the whole of Eastern music from the Mediterranean to
Japan.

New Oxford History of Music, vol. ii: *Early Medieval Music up to 1300,* ed. Dom Anselm Hughes (London, 1954).
The first volume of this publication to appear. The complete work will be in eleven volumes, ranging from the ancient world to the present day. Albums of gramophone records corresponding to the volumes are issued by H.M.V. under the title *The History of Music in Sound,* together with commentaries. The *New Oxford History of Music* is the work of several contributors, English and foreign. There are several illustrations and many music examples, and all foreign texts are supplied with translations. There is a bibliography for each chapter.

New Oxford History of Music, vol. iii: *Ars Nova and the Renaissance,* ed. Dom Anselm Hughes and G. Abraham (London, 1960).
A continuation of vol. ii, carrying the history down to about 1540.

New Oxford History of Music, vol. iv: *The Age of Humanism,* ed. Gerald Abraham (London, 1968).
Covers the period 1540–1630, dealing with secular vocal music, instrumental music, church music and the beginnings of opera.

G. Reese: *Music in the Middle Ages* (New York, 1940).
A comprehensive and thoroughly documented study of the period, including a section on music in the ancient world. There are several illustrations, a substantial number of music examples, and detailed bibliographies for the various chapters.

G. Reese: *Music in the Renaissance* (New York, 1954).
A companion volume to the preceding but twice the size. There is a single bibliography for the whole book and an unusually detailed index. The period covered is roughly from 1400 to 1600.

C. Sachs: *The Rise of Music in the Ancient World* (New York, 1943).
A concise and systematic account of primitive, Oriental, Greek, Roman and Arabian music.

N. Slonimsky: *Music since 1900*, 4th ed. (New York, 1971).
A year-by-year calendar of musical events, often illustrated by press notices and accompanied by pithy comments.

Countries
M. D. Calvocoressi: *A Survey of Russian Music* (London, 1944).
A "Pelican" book, dealing mainly with music in the nineteenth and twentieth centuries.

G. Chase: *The Music of Spain*, 2nd ed. (New York, 1959).

M. Cooper: *French Music from the Death of Berlioz to the Death of Fauré* (London, 1951).

R. Newmarch: *The Music of Czechoslovakia* (London, 1942).
Four out of the fourteen chapters deal with pre-nineteenth-century music.

B. Schwarz: *Music and Musical Life in Soviet Russia, 1917–1970* (London, 1972).

B. Szabolcsi: *A Concise History of Hungarian Music* (London, 1964).
94 pages of text and 126 of music.

E. Walker: *A History of Music in England*, 3rd ed. (Oxford, 1952).
Mainly concerned with music, though there are incidental references to musical conditions. There are 207 music examples and a bibliography.

Forms

E. H. Fellowes: *English Cathedral Music*, 5th ed. (London, 1969).
A survey of music for the Anglican rite from the Reformation
to the twentieth century.

D. J. Grout: *A Short History of Opera*, 2 vols., 2nd ed. (New
York, 1965).
The second volume is devoted to late nineteenth-century and
twentieth-century opera. The documentation of sources is
thorough and there is an extensive bibliography.

A. J. B. Hutchings: *The Baroque Concerto*, 2nd ed. (London,
1963).

W. S. Newman: *The Sonata in the Baroque Era*, 2nd ed. (Chapel
Hill, 1966).
An encyclopedic history of the chamber music of the same
period as the above.

INDEX

A

A cappella, 86
Abraham, Gerald, ix, 110 *n.* 6, 148
  n. 6, 161, 163
Acta Musicologica, 30
Adamberger, Johann Valentin, 117
Addison, Joseph, 33
Adler, Guido, 11
Aelred, Abbot of Rievaulx, 81-2
Agazzari, Agostino, 41
Agincourt song, 92
Agricola, Martin, 40
Albert V, Duke of Bavaria, 90
Alberti family, 32, 96
Algarotti, Francesco, 43
Allen, Warren Dwight, 64 *n.* 3, 160
Ambros, August Wilhelm, 52
Anderson, Emily, 46 *n.* 1, 47 *n.* 12,
  111 *n.* 20, *n.* 39, 133 *n.* 6-9, 134
  n. 25
Anerio, Felice, 55
——Giovanni Francesco, 55
Anne, Queen of England, 32
Anthologie sonore, 31
Antiphonal singing, 74-5
Apel, Willi, 28, 160
Architecture: baroque, 59; Eliza-
  bethan, 72; Gothic, 56, 59, 76
Arnold, Franck Thomas, 47 *n.* 35
——Samuel, 27
Arts Council, 103
Auber, Daniel, 65
Aubry, Pierre, 110 *n.* 11
Aufführungspraxis, 58
Augustus II, King of Poland, 104
——III, King of Poland, 92
Austin, William, 162
Autobiographies of musicians, 36-7
Avison, Charles, 43

B

Bach, Carl Philipp Emanuel: as a
  performer, 37; employed by
  Frederick the Great, 90; keyboard
  concertos, 156; *Versuch über die
  wahre Art das Clavier zu spielen*,
  41; cited, 35, 60
——Johann Sebastian: at Arnstadt,
  83; at Leipzig, 45-6, 79; at Potsdam, 90; use of letter notation, 25;
  playing of chorales, 34; teaching
  of harmony, 41; criticized by
  Scheibe, 42-3; letter to Frederick
  Augustus II, Elector of Saxony,
  92; dispute with the University of
  Leipzig, 104; influence on Romantic composers, 125; cited, 13, 17,
  27, 33, 46 *n.* 3, 53, 57, 59-60, 63,
  68, 117, 127, 131, 142, 145-6,
  153; works:
    Brandenburg concertos, 98,
      116, 141
    cantatas, 21, 77, 79, 86, 114-16,
      155
    Capriccio in B♭, 128
    Ich hatte viel Bekümmernis, 60
    Inventions, 116
    harpsichord concertos, 156
    Italian Concerto, 136, 140
    Mass in B minor, 29, 92
    Musikalisches Opfer, 90, 121
    orchestral suites, 141
    Passion according to St. John,
      21, 77, 79
    Passion according to St. Mat-
      thew, 21, 29, 68, 77, 79, 86,
      113-14, 118
    Was mir behagt, 114
    Wohltemperirte Clavier, Das,
      116